# Theory and Therapy in Dynamic Psychiatry

# Theory and Therapy in Dynamic Psychiatry

## Jules H. Masserman, M.D.

*Professor of Psychiatry and Neurology*
*Northwestern University*

Jason Aronson • New York

Library of Congress Catalog Card Number: 72-96926
Standard Book Number: 0-87668-067-8

Designed by Jennifer Mellen

Manufactured in the United States of America

# Table of Contents

# Table of Cases

# Preface to the Revised Edition

The first version of this manuscript was so well received in academic circles that its present book form, expanded to include recent developments and further fortified by the addition of forty-eight illustrative case histories, may prove of even broader usefulness.

This book is intended to be a brief but inclusive and integrative introduction to psychology and psychiatry, not only for professional students but for all others interested in the dynamics of human behavior and the humane and comprehensive treatment of its individual and cultural deviations.

JULES H. MASSERMAN, M.D.

# Foreword

A professor of psychiatry is a man of many sorrows—not the least of which is that his staff and he must spend a great deal of time in *un*teaching. This is often necessary because not only intelligent laymen but also many advanced students of social work, psychology, sociology, medicine, and related disciplines seem to have acquired, in their earlier college days, concepts of human behavior that were either effectively obscured by outmoded Kraepelinian, Pavlovian, or Freudian jargon—or else simply were not so.

It therefore seemed an act of kindness to all concerned to write this review—mercifully brief, yet hopefully clear and comprehensive—of modern approaches to an understanding of human conduct—its biologic roots, its experiential development, its vicissitudes, and the interrelated physiologic, experiential and social therapies designed to correct undesirable deviations from various "norms" of time, place, and culture.

May it be received in the kindly spirit in which it was written.

JULES H. MASSERMAN, M.D.

To Christine

# Concepts of Personality, Disorder, Disease, and Therapy

No scientific problems can be adequately dealt with until they are meaningfully defined, and this is especially true in the difficult field of human behavior. Fortunately, it is particularly in this sphere that aeons of human experience have left their imprint on the wisdom of our language so that, if we avoid technical jargon, semantic approaches to issues often furnish valuable clues to further clarification. Let us, then, examine the deeper meanings of the key psychiatric terms in the title of this introductory section.

## Concepts of Personality

Among the many meanings of personality, three principal and partially interdependent ones are of therapeutic import:

17

*As a public façade,* the term is derived from *per sona* (through a mouthpiece) denoting the mask behind which an actor in a classical Greek drama could hide while he played an assigned part foreign to his own identity. By psychosociologic implication, many personality problems can be resolved by finding a more suitable and compatible social visage for an essentially unchanged patient.

*Transactionally,* personality comprises combinations of "character traits," each representing a pattern of behavior based on genetic potentials, channeled by life experiences, and, thereafter, expressed in consistent modes of conduct. To change "personality" in this context, the therapist helps the patient develop other latent talents and guides him in exploring newer, more profitable experiences, which are then incorporated into more salutary and effective configurations of conduct.

Related to both definitions is the lay concept of *personality* as a cultural stereotype. For example, the comment "he has a good business personality" often means in our own current culture that the individual referred to is calculating, preemptive, smooth, competitive, opportunistic, and perhaps even dishonest-but-shrewdly-within-the-law. Obviously, an unambitious, modest, retiring, socially "overconscientious" aesthete would have "personality difficulties" in some of our commercial or political enterprises, but in this context it might be contended that it is the social system, not the individual, that needs revision. Cases 1 and 2 illustrate several types of personalities:

CASE 1 The Penurious Man—by Theophrastus (Circa 350 B.C.)

> A Penurious Man is one who goes to a debtor to ask for his half-obol interest before the end of the month. At a dinner where expenses are shared, he counts the number of cups each person drinks, and he makes a smaller libation to Artemis than anyone. If someone has made a good bargain on his account and presents him with the bill, he says it is too much. When his servant breaks a pot or a plate, he deducts the value from his food. If his wife drops a copper, he moves furniture, beds, chests and hunts in the curtains. If he has something to sell he puts such a price on it that the buyer has no profit. He forbids

anyone to pick a fig in his garden, to walk on his land, to pick an olive or a date. Every day he goes to see that the boundary marks of his property have not been moved. He will dun a debtor and exact compound interest. When he entertains the members of his deme, he is careful to serve very small pieces of meat to them. If he goes marketing, he returns without having bought anything. He forbids his wife to lend anything —neither salt nor lamp-wick nor cinnamon nor marjoram nor meals nor garlands nor cakes for sacrifices. "All these trifles," he says, "mount up in a year." To sum up, the coffers of the penurious man are moldy, and the keys rust; they wear cloaks that hardly reach the thigh; a very little oil-bottle supplies them for anointing; they have hair cut short and do not put on their shoes until midday; and when they take their cloak to the fuller, they urge him to use plenty of earth so that it will not be spotted so soon.

CASE 2 Sublimated Reaction Formation

A ruthless financier who had worked his way up from poverty loudly professed his social cynicism and his callousness to the fate of the improvident "rabble of suckers"; nevertheless, to ease his own anxieties, he felt impelled to give large sums of money anonymously to various charitable organizations, libraries, art institutes, etc.

In another case, the reaction formation was even more specific: A man who had made millions by exploiting the domiciliary and occupational needs of Negroes in a large city endowed a foundation dedicated to research on the supposedly obscure causes of interracial resentments and unrest.

## Concepts of Disorder and Disease

Such an appraisal of personality makes more explicit the second and third terms. In effect, *personality disorder* means simply that the person concerned does not fit well into the "order" or system of his time, place, or culture. If the incompatability is particularly severe, it may be called, quite literally, a *dis-ease,* meaning that neither the person nor his society is "at ease" with the other. An interesting corollary to this concept is that there is hardly any deviation that we would call a *neurosis* or a *mental disease* in our culture that in some other setting would be considered not only *normal* (i.e., within the "norms," "mores," or "morals" of another time and place) but also admirable. For example, gentle passivity sometimes to the extreme of masochistic fatalism is advocated by the Zuñi, some Hindu sects, and the Society of Friends; paranoid belligerence and easily aroused violence are wisdom to the Dobuans; epileptic seizures or catatonic stupors are evidences of divine possession in many a religious cult, including some in this country; and throughout the world, what one man regards as ignorance, superstition, and delusional thaumaturgy is another man's holy faith and sacred ritual. This comparative and contingent approach to the concept of "normality" and "adjustment" again introduces an important category of techniques based on the circumstance that a great variety of climates, occupations, and sociocultural environments are available to suit a wide range of individual preferences. To take a whimsical example, an insistent American bigamist could, Mormon Utah being no longer suitable, move to Egypt or Lebanon, become a Muslim, marry four wives, and—provided he conformed to local customs in other respects—live quite "normally" and happily ever after.

## Health

The converse concept of "health" is so composite and contingent that it would be difficult to define if the inherent wisdom of our language were not once again ready at hand. The word itself is derived from the protean Anglo-Saxon root *hal* or *hol*. This root has three principal derivatives in modern English, each charged (or as the psychoanalysts would say, cathected) with deeply humanistic and therapeutic meanings.

1.   From *hal* comes *hale,* connoting physical well-being, strength, and endurance; failing these, *healing,* in the sense of spontaneous recovery or medicosurgical intervention, must take place. Obviously, psychotherapists cannot ever neglect this fundamental biologic basis of *health.*

2. Physical vitality alone, however, does not ensure necessary human alliances; thus, from *hal* also spring *hail, hello* [*heil* in German, *salud* (health to you!) in Spanish, etc.], all having the sense: "Greetings, I wish you well my friend!" Herein lies a deep etymologic recognition that man, as a gregarious, interdependent being, must also cultivate human fellowships. Therefore, a second, equally important meaning of "health" and a corresponding objective of therapy is to guide the patient in developing advantageous social alliances, or to restore them when they have been impaired in his *illness*—a term closely related to the religiocultural concept of *evilness*.

3. From the root *hol* have descended two other associated parameters of meaning: *wholesome* (i.e., integrated and socially approved) and *holy,* denoting an adherence to a local system of beliefs about man's unique worth, his vicarious immortality, and his special place in the universe. In line with this, a final objective of therapy is to help the troubled person regain a sense of personal value integrated with a workable system of mundane and cosmic faiths—whether he calls that system intelligently hedonistic, socially dedicated, or theologically transcendent.

Indeed, in a motivational sense these terms are operationally interchangeable, since the scientist, the humanitarian, and the pietist, like the more frankly sensual hedonist, all seek personal rewards and fulfillments, though through somewhat different modalities and procedures. Whether or not the therapist accepts this egalitarian appraisal (the patient usually does not), it is an important function of therapy to help the patient find that system of faiths and practices within the range of cultural compatability that will best serve his needs for significance and security.

## Concepts of Therapy and Cure

Therapy is derived from the Greek *therapeuien,* the root meaning of which is "service"—and serving the best interests of a fellow human being, whether stranger, friend, client, or patient, is the purpose of all treatment as well as the hallmark of civilization. Significantly, also, the word *cure* is related to Latin *curare*—to care for. But in the context of therapy, a stranger or a friend is distinguished from a "client" or "patient" in that the latter is directly or indirectly forced by society to seek help for a "personality disorder" in various contexts outlined above.

In this preliminary survey of the rationale and objectives of therapy, we have thus far avoided the prefix *psycho* because of the misleading mystique generally associated with it. In the Greek legend, Psyche was a mortal maiden who was justly punished for her *hubris* in flouting her secret lover's wishes and detecting that he was the god Eros—a charming parable, but what with various "instincts," "complexes," and "conflicts" named after Narcissus, Electra, Oedipus *et al.*, we already have too many eponymic myths in the field. In addition, the literal translations of *psyche* as "mind" or "soul" are equally intangible, since we deal with active human beings and not with nebulous Platonic abstractions. Operationally, "mind" is not a *thing* but a verb denoting various observable bodily functions: We "mind" in the process of attending, sensing, and perceiving; we are "reminded" when we utilize previous experiences in a changing context; and we "mind" in the sense of obeying physical necessities and sociocultural directives. Indeed, we can know a person's "mind" *only* by his behavior, including the behavior of his internal organs that we call physiology or psychosomatics, or that of his vocal cords, palate, tongue, and teeth that we call speech.[1]

This further clarifies our threefold therapeutic task. If the body is handicapped by physical disease, and especially if this impairs the sensory, mnemonic, associative, and motor capacities of the central nervous system, *effective therapy must include restoring these*

---

[1] We need not, however, subscribe to the oversimplified stimulus–response concepts of a formerly popular school of psychology called *Behaviorism*, as applied to therapy by "reciprocal inhibition" (see p. 177).

*functions to normal by medical or surgical means insofar as possible.* In addition, if the patient has also developed culturally inappropriate behavior, we must (a) *help him learn by re-examination, analysis, and revaluation that his past and current patterns of aberrant conduct are neither as necessary nor as advantageous as he has, consciously or not, assumed them to be* and (b) *guide him toward newer modes of social adaptation that, through further experience, he will choose to maintain as ultimately more practicable and profitable.* Finally, these readaptations will include more realistic humanitarian and religious cognitions, thus completing the triune essence of somatically restorative, socially habilitative, and intellectually reorientating therapy.

As may be inferred from the above, three corresponding modalities of therapy have emerged: organic–individual, socio-cultural, and religiophilosophic, with many "schools" in each category. Moreover, each school[1] and subschool has advocated a separate theoretic system in a new terminology (or worse, attributed different meanings to the same terms) and attempted to prescribe supposedly unique methods of therapy on the presumption that they were more "scientific," "efficient," or "fundamental" than those based on older concepts. The facts of the matter, however, are these: Ever since Esquirol's classic study in 1838, *Des Maladies Mentales,* comprehensive and objective reviews by Fiedler, Levitt, Frank, Eysenck, and many others have shown that whereas every rational method of therapy produces some relief of symptoms—else it would not remain long in use—the eventual results are approximately the same for all and disconcertingly little better than for control subjects. In effect, about a third of those treated by any method—or by none—consider themselves in various degrees "recovered," another third improved, and the rest unimproved or worse. These startling statistics can be accounted for by variations on two main hypotheses:

---

[1] *School* is a word more appropriate to mindless aggregations of fish than to thoughtful scientists.

1. All formal therapies are only partially and temporarily effective and, therefore, scarcely worth the effort.

2 Whatever their theoretic formulations, all therapies exploit fundamentally the same modes of recovery that are evoked, albeit somewhat later, by spontaneously rehabilitative experiences in the nontreated—hence the more immediate improvement after formal therapy but the close similarity of long-term results in the "treated" and "untreated" groups.

The claims of competing theories and therapeutic techniques can then be further accounted for by the circumstance that each "school" attracts and suits its own practitioners and adherents who, sharing a common enthusiasm for a theory and a method, bolster each other's personal, intellectual, and social securities.

Fortunately, in the reassuring dyadic relationship formed between any effective therapist and receptive "patient" (or "client"), the former helps the latter face his realistic problems and, admittedly or not, guides him toward practicable solutions. In this sense, it matters relatively little on what theoretic bases these solutions were formulated or if a correspondingly "correct" drug, shock, or "psychologic" therapy had been used: e.g., whether the patient had ingested the exact dose of phenothiazine, had suffered an adequate number of convulsions, had analyzed his Freudian "castration fears," had compensated for his Adlerian "inferiority complex," had explored his Jungian "atavistic unconscious," or had attained a state of Zen *satori*. Indeed, a skeptical observer might define these various brands of supposedly essential experiences and "insights" as temporarily happy states in which the therapist and patient had come to share the same comforting illusions. However, if the observer were also scientifically inclined, he would then try to discern *what elements common to the various modes of therapy—and present to a lesser but important extent in spontaneous experience* —were operative in effecting improvement.

Under these circumstances, further partisan debate among the advocates of various contending theories and methodologies serves little purpose; instead, recourse must be had to correlated biologic research and controlled clinical observations designed to investigate (a) the causes f aberrant behavior (termed, according to increasing deviation from the norm, "idiosyncratic," "neurotic," "psycho-pathic," or "psychotic") and (b) the essential factors in various pro-cedures that are operative in restoring "normal" (more effectively and lastingly adaptive) conduct.

# Experimental Approaches

As conducted at Northwestern University for the past quarter century, our own investigations in this field have led to the formulation of four basic biodynamic principles that correlate animal and human, "normal" and "abnormal" behavior as follows:

1. *Principle of Motivational Development.* All behavior originates in variably emergent physiologic needs for nutrition, fluids, manipulative locomotion, parental conduct, etc., among which, parenthetically, sexual gratifications are relatively episodic, transient, and dispensable.
2. *Principle of Learned Individuation.* Each organism's evolving patterns of adaptation are unique resultants of (a) its innate

potentialities, (b) its various modes and rates of maturation, and (c) its individual experiences.

3.  *Principle of Equivalent Adaptability.* Most frustrations and dissatisfactions are adequately met by a versatile repertoire of (a) readjusted techniques or (b) substitutive goals.

4.  *Principle of Conflictual Uncertainty in Neurotigenesis.* Marked and persistent deviation of behavior can be induced by stressing any organism between mutually incompatible patterns of adaptation: as, for instance, subjecting a cat to an unpredictable electric shock during conditioned feeding, or requiring a monkey to secure food from a box in which, on several occasions, he had *unexpectedly* been confronted with a toy snake—an object as representationally dangerous to the monkey as a live one, harmless or not, would be. Yet, counter to classical Freudian or Wolpean doctrines, "fear" in the sense of dread of injury need not be involved at all; equally serious and lasting neurotigenic effects can be induced by facing the animal with difficult choices among mutually exclusive satisfactions— situations that parallel the disruptive effects of prolonged hesitations among equally attractive alternatives in human affairs. In other modes of inducing uncertainties, variably delayed feedbacks of the animal's own vocalizations or irregularly timed or sensorially confused cues as to impending electroshocks can also render an animal's milieu unpredictable and thereby anxiety-provoking and neurotigenic. Any of these stresses, when they exceed the subject's adaptive capacities, induce physiologic and mimetic manifestations of anxiety, spreading inhibitions, generalizing phobias, stereotyped rituals, "psychosomatic" dysfunctions, impaired social interactions, addictions to alcohol and other drugs, regressions to immature patterns of behavior, cataleptic stupors, and other marked and persistent deviations of conduct.

These principles were derived from the following data.

# Principle I. Motivational Development

PHASES

Our studies have confirmed the premise that the young of all animals, including man, pass through an orderly succession of stages, during which sensory modalities are distinguished, integrated concepts of the environment are developed, manipulative skills are refined, early dependencies are relinquished in favor of exploration and mastery, and peer and sexual relationships are sought through which the individual becomes normally "socialized" in its group. In continued studies over the past twenty years, the growth of animals of various species from infancy to adulthood has been carefully recorded and progressively photographed in motion pictures. Our observations have revealed the following important influences, again with significant clinical counterparts.

EARLY DEPRIVATION

Young animals subjected to periods of solitary confinement, though otherwise physically well cared for, do not develop normal initiative, physical stamina, or appropriate social behavior, apparently because of inadequate stimuli during critical periods of growth and receptivity.

FORMATIVE EXPERIENCES

Conversely, young animals provided with the necessary nutritive, protective, and guiding presence of adults, supplemented by play and other contacts with peers, acquire self-confidence, motor skills, and social "acculturations."

# Principle II. Learned Individuation: "Personality"

The growing animal infants show patterns of dependency, exploration, fetishism (i.e., attachment to objects such as nipples or blankets representing early securities), rebelliousness, nascent sexuality, and other characteristics significantly parallel to those in human children. Concurrently, any surrogate parents involved, whether of the animal's own species or not, impart their own traits to the adopted young. For example, a young rhesus monkey, raised from birth in the investigator's home, learned to respond with surprising sensitivity and adequacy to human language and action, but never acquired some of the patterns (e.g., a fear of snakes) "normal" to rhesus monkeys raised by their own mothers.

## CHARACTER DEVIANCE

Unusual early experiences may thus engram peculiar characteristics that persist through adulthood. For example, if a young animal is taught to work a pedal switch that administers increasingly intense, but tolerable, electric shocks as a necessary preliminary to securing food, as an adult it may continue to seek such shocks even in the absence of any other immediate reward, and may thus appear to be inexplicably *masochistic* to an observer unacquainted with its special early history. So, also, if a young animal is subjected to exceedingly severe conflicts between mutually exclusive satisfactions, counterposed desires and aversions, or environments that pose threats beyond its capacities to predict or control, it develops deeply ingrained inhibitions, fears, rituals, somatic disorders, social maladjustments, and other aberrations of behavior that become highly elaborate and more difficult to treat than those similarly precipitated in adulthood.

## EARLY BRAIN INJURIES

A remarkable finding was that adequate care and training in early life could, in large part, compensate for extensive brain damage in the newborn. Monkeys subjected to the removal of both temporal or parietal cortices at birth, but given a protective and stimulating home environment thereafter, suffered minor kinesthetic and affective impairments detectable by specific tests or by periods of sensory deprivation, yet developed otherwise normal and adequate individual and social adaptations. On the other hand, in the absence of such special care and training, the effects of brain damage, including lesions in the thalami, amygdalae, and in cerebral areas 13,

23, and 24 were much more devastating in the young than in adult animals. In this connection also, cerebral lesions in young animals did not ameliorate induced experimental neuroses as effectively as in the case of adults.

# Principle III. Range of Adaptability

GROUP ORGANIZATION

Our studies have supplemented the observations of ethologists by demonstrating that animal societies in the laboratory as well as in the wild (or civilized?) state organize themselves in hierarchies of relatively dominant and submissive members, with leadership and privilege generally preempted not by size or strength alone but in accordance with special aptitudes, skills, and other "personality" characteristics. These social relationships could be modified in the following significant ways:

COOPERATION

Under special experimental conditions, a cat or a monkey could be trained to operate a mechanism that produced food for a partner, who then reciprocated in "mutual service."

PARASITISM

In most pairings, however, this pattern soon deteriorated into either (a) a situation in which both animals would rather starve than work for each other or (b) a relationship in which one animal (the "worker") operated the mechanism sufficiently frequently to feed both himself and a "dependent" or "social parasite."

TECHNOLOGICAL SOLUTIONS

Two such workers, among fourteen pairs, were sufficiently "intelligent" (i.e., possessed of unusually high perceptive–manipulative capacities) to jam the feeding mechanism so that it operated automatically, rendering further effort by either partner unnecessary.

"ALTRUISM"

Some social animals in our studies were capable of spontaneous "self-sacrificing" conduct without apparent reward other than that of preventing discomfort or pain to another member of the colony. For example, a macaque monkey would starve for hours rather than pull a lever to secure readily available food, if it had learned that this act would subject another macaque to an electric shock. This "succoring" behavior was apparently less dependent upon the relative age, size, or sex of the two animals than on (a) their individual "character" and (b) whether or not they had been mutually well-adjusted cagemates.

AGGRESSION

Conversely, *aggression* in the sense of actual fighting among members of the same species to establish various relationships was minimal; primacy and dexterity manifested by only occasional gestures of preemption were nearly always sufficient to establish dominance and privileges. Indeed, physical combat appeared only under the following special circumstances:

1. When an animal accustomed to a high position in its own group was transferred to one in which it came into direct conflict with new rivals previously accustomed to dominance.
2. When a tyrannical animal was subjected to an unexpected rebellion by an alliance of subordinates.
3. When a female with increased status derived from mating with a high-ranking male turned on members of her group that had previously oppressed her.
4. When a dominant animal, by being made experimentally neurotic (*v.i.*), fell to a low position in its group and thereafter expressed its frustrations by physical attacks on both inanimate and living objects in its environment.

In effect, such experiments helped clarify the biodynamic interrelationships basic to partnerships, sit-down strikes, contracts and automation, altruism and hostility expressed with far greater complexity in human society.

## Principle IV. Neurotigenesis

### METHODS OF INDUCTION

These consisted of subjecting the animal to motivational–adaptational conflicts in situations in which its coping capacities could no longer produce predictably satisfactory solutions. This resulted in deviant patterns of avoidance, substitution, ritualization, regression, and other aberrant modes of conduct. The procedures follow.

#### INDUCTION OF AN EXPERIMENTAL NEUROSIS

A cat (or a rat, dog, or monkey) is trained to respond to the flash of a light or the sound of a bell by opening a box to secure a pellet of food. It is then further trained to depress a switch to operate these feeding-signals at will. During the period of training, the animal is friendly to the experimenter, enters the training cage eagerly, and operates the switch readily and effectively; indeed, the animal sometimes continues to do so even after its hunger is satiated. When the feeding responses are prevented by disconnecting the switch, interposing barriers, locking the food-box, or failing to drop the food after the signals, the animal indulges in substitutive behavior such as striking the disk switch vigorously or sitting on it, reaching for the lights, reexploring the cage, playing with the wires and barriers, or attempting to attract the experimenter by approaching as close as the cage will permit and scratching or mewing for attention. Soon, however, the animal adapts to the new situation by ignoring the signals and the food-box, although without developing any signs of aversion to the switch, the signals, the cage or the experimenter. Moreover, the animal can easily be retrained to abandon its substitutive activities and resume working the switch whenever the food-reward is again made regularly available.

If, however, on several irregularly spaced occasions the animal is permitted to work the switch and reach for the food, but is at that moment poised between mutually exclusive rewards, given a mild, physiologically harmless, but *unexpected* airblast or electric shock or is subjected to other vectors of unpredictability, the situation obviously becomes motivationally conflictful or charged with uncertainty. The switch–signal configuration still represents the possibility of satisfying hunger, providing the animal responds with its learned adaptive behavior of taking the food deposited in the box, but the same configuration now also threatens the animal with a dilemma of choice, an unpleasant experience or a traumatic failure of control. Under these circumstances, remarkable changes in the total behavior of the animal occur in prototypes that so clearly correspond to neurotic patterns in the human that, for purposes of comparison, the two classes of observation may be juxtaposed under the following headings.

*Anxiety.* The animal crouches, trembles, shows horripilation, dilated pupils and retracted nictitating membranes, breathes rapidly, shallowly, and irregularly, but has a fast, pounding pulse and a markedly increased blood pressure. Special studies reveal increased epinephrine and 17-ketosteroid content and gastorintestinal stasis, diminished clotting time, and other bodily changes indicative of the mobilization of various physiologic resources and "emergency mechanisms." These manifestations of motor and sympathetic tension, then, parallel those that accompany the subjective experience of normal and neurotic anxiety in the human.

*Phobias, Startle Reactions, and Hypersensitivity to Stimuli.* The manifestations of anxiety increase markedly when the light or bell signals are given, when the animal is forced toward the food-box by a movable barrier, or when, though hungry, it is offered food pellets similar to those that it formerly secured in the box. Moreover, these aversions quickly become more generalized: The animal resists being put into the experimental cage and immediately attempts to escape from it; it avoids the experimental room and, in many cases, the experimenter himself. Similarly, when it is replaced in its accustomed home cage, it shows severe startle reactions and phobic aversions to sudden lights or sounds, to constricted spaces or to restraint, and especially to any sensory stimuli in the modality associated with its "traumatic experience," e.g., the click of an electric switch or even the scarcely perceptible sound of an insect sprayer.

*Inhibitions and Repressions.* Animals with severe experimental neuroses may refuse to take food in or out of the experimental cage and may, indeed, starve themselves into a state of morbid inanition. Those with less severe neuroses will show incomplete inhibitions of feeding: They will eat only food pellets of a shape or composition other than those used in the experiment ("food faddism") or they will feed spontaneously only if outside the experimental or home cage. Another type of inhibition of activity is highly suggestive of a process of "repression." For example, neurotic cats that do not actively avoid the feeding switch will treat it as if they had never known its function; in contrast to their pre-neurotic eagerness to reach it, they will walk around or over it as if they were hardly aware of its presence. In animals only mildly neurotic, phobic reactions to the light or bell may be replaced by a similar behavioral "amnesia" for the previously well-learned significance of these stimuli as signals for food.

*Motor Disturbances and Compulsive Behavior.* An animal with a severe experimental neurosis may show gross aberrations of motor function, ranging from cataleptic immobility to continuous, apparently aimless hyperactivity. Between these extremes lie patterns with more specific counterphobic or "compulsive" content: A hungry neurotic animal may invariably hide its head "counterphobically" in the food-box in response to a feeding signal, yet refuse to eat; another may turn on its back and claw at the light in a symbolically defensive manner; a third will show aversion amounting to fear of a caged mouse that has been placed in the experimental cage during the neurotigenic experiment. One neurotic dog developed the ritual of circling the food-box three times and then bowing on its forepaws before attempting to feed.

*"Psychosomatic" Disturbances and "Organ Neuroses."* Many animals show disturbances of gastrointestinal function in the form of diarrhea or constipation, stools indicative of internal bleeding, and a persistent loss of weight. More specific "organ neurotic" dysfunctions may also occur: pulse irregularities, polydipsia and frequent urination, ejaculatio praecox, and an increased susceptibility to serious eye and skin infections.

*Regressive Behavior.* This was indicated by a tendency to isolation, decreased interest in sexual activities, and surrender of dominance in the group hierarchy. Similarly, cats often showed an excessive preoccupation with interminable licking and preening, contrasted with a carelessness in the disposition of excreta that is rare among normal domesticated animals of this species. Neurotic animals also showed "regressive" changes in their "transference" relationships to the experimenter; they became either unpredictably aggressive, or much more frequently, reverted to a prehensile clinging sometimes accompanied by nestling and nursing movements.

CONSTITUTIONAL INFLUENCES

Animals closest to man showed symptoms most nearly resembling those in human neuroses and psychoses, but in each case the "neurotic syndrome" manifested depended less on the nature of the conflict (which could be held constant) than on the *constitutional predisposition* of the animal. For example, under similar stresses spider monkeys reverted to infantile dependencies or catatonic immobility, Cebus developed various "psychosomatic disturbances, including functional paralyses, whereas vervets became diffusely aggressive, persisted in bizarre sexual patterns, or preferred hallucinatory satisfactions such as chewing and swallowing purely imaginary meals while avoiding real food to the point of self-starvation.

# Techniques of Therapy

Equally germane to our clinical interests were the procedures that proved to be most effective in ameliorating or eliminating the deviations of behavior induced by the experimental stresses. Five *psychosocial* and three *physical* methods analogous to those in clinical therapy can be summarized.

PSYCHOSOCIAL MODALITIES

CHANGE OF MILIEU

A neurotic animal given a prolonged rest (three to twelve months) in a favorable home environment nearly always showed relief from the somatic manifestations of anxiety and tension and a diminution of phobic–compulsive, aggressive, and regressive behavior. These neurotic patterns were prone to reappear, however, when the animal was returned to the laboratory, even though it was not again subjected to a direct repetition of conflictual experiences. To draw a human parallel, a soldier with severe "battle neurosis" resulting from an impasse between duty and fear may appear "recovered" after a restful sojourn in a base hospital. But unless his conflictual attitudes are resolved, his symptoms and his escapist or other reactions to latent anxiety will again become severe when he is returned to combat.

SATIATION OF A CONFLICTUAL NEED

If a neurotically self-starved animal that had refused food for two days was forcibly tube-fed and its hunger thus mitigated, its neurotic manifestations correspondingly decreased. Hippocrates is reported by Soranus (perhaps apocryphally) to have utilized a corresponding method for resolving a marital impasse. Hippocrates, it seems, was once called into consultation to treat a strange hypertonic and convulsive malady that was keeping a recent bride virginal. Discerning, after a private interview, that she was torn between strong sexual desires neatly countered by fears of defloration, Hippocrates advised the husband "to light the torch of Hymen," with or without the patient's consent. The results, though not recorded, were presumed to be mutually satisfactory.

ENVIRONMENTAL PRESS

A hungry, neurotic cat, dog, or monkey was constricted closer and closer to the feeder until its head was almost in contact with a profusion of delectable pellets. Under such circumstances, some animals, despite their fears, suddenly lunged for the food; thereafter they needed lesser degrees of "environmental press" until their feeding-inhibition disappeared altogether, carrying other neurotic generalizations with it. This method is a variation of the Hippocratic (currently "behavioral" or "gestalt") mode of pressure, but entails a more crucial response on the part of the patient. In some ways, the procedure is akin to forcing a boy afraid of water to enter a shallow pool. Depending upon his *capacities for reintegrating his experiences* (in analytic terms, his "ego strength"), he may find that there was, after all, no cause for fear; conversely, however, he may react with abject terror and thereafter hate not only the water, but pools, swimming—and all future therapists. Because of the latter eventuality, ruthless coercion is generally considered a dangerous method in dealing with neurotic anxieties.

SOCIAL INFLUENCES

An inhibited, phobic animal placed with others that respond normally to the experimental situation will show some amelioration of its neurotic patterns, although never to the degree of complete "recovery." In like manner, problem children do better when they have an opportunity to live with "normal" youngsters in an environment that favors "normality," although more specific individual therapy is often necessary to foster the "cure."

SPONTANEOUS REEXPLORATION

Some animals will gradually retest the use of the switch and feeding mechanism without external constriction, take the food, and concurrently dispel other neurotic inhibitions and deviations of intra-group conduct at their own pace. So, also, most human beings will spontaneously and providentially reexplore and reassert their mastery over the residues of most traumatic physical or social experiences without direct compulsion, need for therapy, or benefit of clergy.

REEDUCATION BY A TRUSTED MENTOR

If, however, spontaneous recovery does not occur, directed, graduated guidance can be effective. As noted, a neurotic animal, perhaps by the very virtue of its regression to earlier patterns of relationship, becomes exceedingly dependent upon the experimenter for protection and care. If this trust is not violated, the experimenter may then retrain the animal by gentle steps: first, to take food from his hand; next, to accept food in the apparatus; then, to open the box while the experimenter merely hovers protectively; and finally, to work the switch and feed as formerly without further "support" from the "therapist." During its "rehabilitation," the animal not only reexplores and resolves its motivational conflicts but also masters and dissipates the symbolic generalizations that spring from this nuclear "complex," i.e., the inhibitions, phobias, compulsions, and other neurotic reactions. This, indeed, may be the paradigm for the basic processes in much clinical psychotherapy. The neurotic patient channels his needs for help toward a therapist onto whom he transfers his dependent and other relationships. The therapist then utilizes this "transference" with optimal patience and wisdom to guide and support the patient as the latter reexamines his conflictual desires and fears, recognizes his previous misinterpretation of reality, and essays new ways of living until he is sufficiently successful and confident to proceed on his own. Whether this be called reeducation, retraining, psychotherapy, psychoanalysis, or rehabilitation depends more on the context of the problem, the necessity for thoroughness in anamnestic review and symbolic analysis, and the skill and effectiveness in the utilization of the fantasied and actual interpersonal relationships involved than on any fundamental differences in the essential dynamics of the respective procedures.

PHYSICAL METHODS

In addition to the individual, dyadic, and social modalities described, physical methods such as the use of drugs, electroshock, and neurosurgery have also proved clinically advantageous in the treatment of behavior disorders. Their experimental parallels may be reviewed briefly:

ACTIONS OF DRUGS

Preliminary tests of the effects of various sedative and narcotic drugs on normal animals showed that, in general, alcohol, bromides, barbiturates, opiates, and, less efficiently, various meprobamate phenothiazine or other "tranquilizers" disorganized complex behavior patterns, while they left simple ones relatively intact. Thus, in one series of experiments an animal was taught in successive stages: (1) to open a food box, (2) to respond to food signals, including signs reading FOOD or NO FOOD, (3) to operate the signal switch, (4) to work several switches in a given order, and finally (5) to traverse a difficult maze to reach one of the switches. If the animal was then drugged with a small dose of barbital, morphine, or alcohol, it would become incapable of solving the maze but would still work the food switches properly; with larger doses, it could "remember" how to work only one switch; with still larger doses, earlier stages of learning would also be disintegrated until finally it lost even the simple skill required to open the reward box. Conversely, as the animal recovered from its intoxication, its learned responses were reconstitutued in their original order. If now the animal were made neurotic as outlined above, it developed a new set of highly intricate and elaborate reactions: the various inhibitions, phobias, compulsions, somatic dysfunctions, and sensorimotor disturbances previously described. These also proved relatively more vulnerable to pharmacologic disintegration than did the simpler, pretraumatic behavior patterns; if a neurotic animal were given barbital or morphine, its anxiety reactions and inhibitions were significantly relieved. In effect, instead of crouching tense and immobile in a far corner or showing panic at the feeding signals, it could respond to the latter by opening the box and feeding (in a somewhat groggy but comparatively effective manner) as though, for the time being, its doubts and fears were wraiths forgotten.

*Drug Addiction.* In one variant of these studies in which alcohol was used as the nepenthic drug, the animals that experienced relief from neurotic tensions while partly intoxicated were later given an opportunity to choose between alcohol and nonalcoholic drinks. To our surprise (and, it may be admitted, covert delight) about half the neurotic animals in these experiments began to develop a quite unfeline preference for alcohol; moreover, in most cases the proclivity was sufficiently insistent and prolonged to warrant the term *addiction*. In further proof of its neurotic basis, the induced dipsomania generally lasted until the animal's underlying neurosis was relieved by one or more of the psychosocial methods of therapy described. It seems redundant to discuss the human analogies to these experimental observations.

*"Protective" Effects.* In still another series of experiments, we observed that the administration of alcohol so dulled the perceptive and mnemonic capacities of animals that they were, while thus inebriated, relatively immune to the neurosis-producing effects of traumatic experiences. In this connection it may be recalled that many a human being has been tempted to take a "bracer" before bearding the boss, getting married, flying a combat mission, or facing other presumed dangers including those of social conviviality or the mystique of religious rituals.

CEREBRAL ELECTROSHOCK

When a 35-volt, 60-cycle alternating current, such as is usually employed in clinical electroconvulsive therapy, was passed through the brain of an animal for two seconds, the resultant cortical diaschisis also served to disintegrate complex and recently acquired patterns of behavior, whether these were "normal" or "neurotic." Unlike most drugs, however, *electroshock* produced permanent impairment, however subtle, of future behavioral efficiency, even when this defect could not be correlated with pathologic changes in the brain detectable by present methods. Weaker or modified currents (the direct-wave *Leduc* type) produced lesser degrees of cerebral disorganization in our animals, but also had less effect on their neurotic behavior. All in all, these experiments supported the growing conviction among psychiatrists that electroshock and other drastic therapies may be useful in certain relatively recent and acute psychoses, but that the neuronal damage they produce, however covert, makes their indiscriminate use replete with partially hidden defects and potential danger.

LOBOTOMY, TOPECTOMY, THALAMOTOMY

Obviously, any cerebral operation will (a) produce a transient general disruption of response patterns that may be temporarily desirable and (b) result in a more circumscribed hiatus in the patient's reactive capacities—both effects of possible therapeutic import. Indeed, recent studies by a number of workers, especially Bard, Pribram, Delgado, Rioch, and others (see Bibliography) have revealed new possibilities for altering basic patterns of behavior by specific cerebral lesions. Thus, section of the head of the caudate or under Area 13 in the posterior orbital gyrus may counteract otiosity and release spontaneity and responsive activity, although the latter may sometimes take the form of vicious rage. Conversely, lesions in the ventral thalmic-cingulate-hippocampal-amygdaloid circuits of the "visceral brain" may tame destructive and aggressive behavior, though perhaps at the cost of peculiarly regressive patterns in which the animal mouths everything within reach yet fails to learn from adverse experience. Work in our own laboratory has indicated that circumscribed lesions in the thalamus and in the amygdalae may disintegrate experimentally induced neurotic patterns and over-balance the corresponding organic loss in adaptive skills by a sufficiently wide margin, so that from the standpoint of survival and apparent contentment, the animal is undoubtedly benefited. Some of these findings are being tested clinically by Scoville, Dax and Radley-Smith, Grantham, and others, in cerebral operations designed specifically for various forms of psychotic behavior. One qualification, however, is of basic significance: *the effects of apparently identical lesions in different animals vary with their individual previous experiences*—a circumstance that underlines once again the necessity for dealing with each organism, from the standpoint of both etiology and therapy, as a uniquely evolved bio-dynamic entity. To apply this to the human, each person behaves differently from every other because (a) he was differently constituted at birth, and (b) he has had different experiences. Therefore, (1) he will react uniquely to any given cerebral lesion, and (2) he will then need rehabilitative therapy specially tailored to fit his frame and mode of action, compensate for his defects, and best utilize his remaining capacities for optimal adaptation.

## Significance of Animal Research

The question that still occasionally arises at this juncture—though, thanks be, far less frequently than formerly—is usually phrased somewhat as follows: "But are not these inferences from animal experiments *anthropomorphized?* Indeed, are they *really* (sic) relevant to human conduct which, as some of us have been taught, is so completely bound up with arcane conations such as *narcissism, libido* vs. *thanatos,* or higher-order abstractions such as aesthetic, moral, and spiritual values? These will be more fully dealt with in later clinical sections, but here in brief:

First, epistemologically, since all data, "natural" or "experimental," can be called indistinguishably "objective" or "subjective," and since all abstractions, inferences, theorems, and conclusions are molded only in human thought, the terms *real* and *anthropomorphic* become tautologic shibboleths, meaningless to modern heuristics.

Second, neuropsychologically, just as the central nervous system of *homo habilis* is more highly developed *but of the same basic design as* that of "lower" mammals, so also is human behavior more highly dependent on communicative and social influences and *thereby more complex and contingent--but not different in basic adaptational patterns than* the behavior of man's less pretentious, preemptive, and warlike fellow creatures. Nevertheless, since these are merely logical statements incompatible with the remnants of man's pre-Copernican and pre-Darwinian arrogance, some of us will continue to cherish the proud conviction that man's body and behavior are completely unique—and, therefore, "so are his neuroses."

## Man's Principal Distinction from Other Animals: His Delusions and Ur-Defenses

In the preceding section, we briefly reviewed the leads culled from comparative and experimental psychology relevant to biodynamic theory and therapy. Undeniably, however, men *do* differ from animals (a) in the complexity and versatility with which human beings elaborate both "normal" and "neurotic" behavior and (b) in several transcendent articles of faith (or illusions?) that may exist in animals only in larval form. In anticipation of later discussions, these ultimate (Ur-) assumptions and beliefs comprise:

1. *The Ur-delusion of personal invulnerability, power, and literal or vicarious immortality,* rooted in a sense of primary being and never surrendered.

2. *The Ur-tenet of "trust in humanity,"* derived from the almost equally illogical presumption that because one's mother at one time loved and cherished one, the rest of mankind must be almost equally provident and cooperative. This expectation of survival through interdependence, when combined with dominative, erotic, and other yearnings, determines many of our interpersonal and sociocultural transactions, including the relationships of patient and therapist.

3. *The Ur-search for a perfect wisdom that can discern order and security in a universe of chaos and danger.* This can be accomplished by the invention of wishfully inclusive "sciences" or "philosophies"—or, when these fail, by a regressive reliance on the intercession of omnipotent and omniscient Beings who can be controlled by wheedling, bribery, or command much as one once controlled one's parents.

In further preview, then:

1. Consciously or not, each of us strives for physical survival, social belonging, and cosmic identity. However, each person's modes of seeking these goals depend on his endowments and change with his maturity and experience, so that all human imagery, communication, and action vary greatly with clime, time, and culture.

2. Frustration and conflict in any essential aspect of adaptation—

physical, social, or philosophic—can give rise to subjective anxieties, physical dysfunctions, and social maladaptations.

3.  The aberrations of conduct so induced are approved, tolerated, or rejected differently by various cultures in a continuous range that extends from "normal" or "idiosyncratic" through the "neurotic" and "sociopathic" to the "psychotic."

4.  Finally, the amelioration or "cure" of these deviations lies not in a merely verbal encounter between "patient" and "therapist" but what this *im*plies—yet often does not *su*pply: first, eliminating, insofar as possible, the patient's physical handicaps; second, imparting to him by every interpersonal and social means at the therapist's command the recognition that his deviant patterns of inhibition, avoidance, substitution, aggression, flight, etc., are not really as necessary as he had assumed. At the same time the therapist guides the patient toward other modes of conduct that will not only be considered more "normal" (compensable) by society, but that he himself will eventually find more pleasurable and profitable. Third, the therapist also helps the patient deduce a system of beliefs and a culturally practicable philosophy of life in which he can find comfort and serenity.

# Interview Techniques and Diagnostic Objectives

This section will deal briefly with the most important initial step in the therapy of the personality disorders: the "diagnostic" (Greek— thorough understanding) interview (i.e., interchange of viewpoints). The following suggestions as to the sensitivity, tact, and skill necessary to establish essential rapport will help elicit the required information in a reasonably short time and promote later therapy.

## Methods

Assure the subject that his confidence will be respected, and adhere to this except when overriding dangers of suicide or violence require his own protection or that of others.

If he employs the usual evasive euphemisms, induce him gently to specify *under what circumstances* he develops what he calls "nervousness," "muscle tension," "dizziness," "spells of worry," "strange feelings," etc.; however, do not press too hard if he is obviously resistive to more searching inquiry. As he becomes more cooperative and specific, invite him to discuss in greater detail various situations in which he is most likely to be anxious, phobic, obsessional, depressed, or enraged, to take recourse to alcohol or drugs as described below—or, conversely, when he is least likely to do so. Throughout this inquiry, the particular stresses that precipitated the "present illness" are especially significant. Gentle questions along these lines are rarely resented and may be highly illuminating, not only as to the nature and psychologic relationships of the patient's past and current neurotic, psychosomatic (see p. 94 ff.), characterologic, or even psychotic difficulties, but also as to the latent strengths and assets that may be utilized in his therapy.

Eventually, although not necessarily at the first interview, tactful explorations of the patient's ethnic background and his early familial, social, educational, sexual, occupational, and other formative experiences (the psychiatric history) may afford further valuable perspectives as to his current potentials as well as his past vulnerabilities and furnish even broader perspective for treatment.[1] Urgent imperatives in the patient's plea for help must be implemented by medical or, if necessary, institutional care.

## Syndromes

The therapist should remember from periods of intense strain and worry in his own life that what the patient describes may represent many diverse combinations of physical and mental distress, rather than a diagnosis that is in spurious accord with some pejorative psychologic or psychiatric label. Nevertheless, a few kindly, evocative questions may elicit consistent descriptions of one or more of the following *syndromes,* which represent the most frequent reactions to stress and uncertainty.

---

[1] For a more detailed guide see Masserman, J. and Schwab, J.: *The Psychiatric Interview*, Grune and Stratton, 1973.

## Anxiety States

These are relatively acute episodes of unformulated but intense subjective apprehension, accompanied physically by cardiac palpitation, catchy respiration, pounding pulse, laryngeal spasm (*globus hystericus*), sweating, tremulousness, "butterflies in the stomach" (due to splanchnic constriction), urinary urgency, and other symptoms of psychosomatic imbalance. Often gratuitously diagnosed by the sufferer as "heart attacks" or "fainting spells," these episodes characteristically occur when he feels himself faced with harrowing doubts as to whether he can cope with serious threats to his physical, cultural, or philosophic securities: a suddenly evoked fear of disease or death, or of social isolation, or of the loss of a cherished faith. Fortunately, such acute reactions indicate latent vitality and mobility, so that helping the anxious individual to clarify and dispel the sources of his intense apprehension may bring dramatic subjective and symptomatic relief.

CASE 3 Erotogenic Anxiety Syndrome

A twenty-eight-year-old married woman, whose husband had entered the army eight months previously, applied for the treatment of "heart trouble" because of attacks of heart-pounding, fainting, giddiness, and trembling. These attacks, she stated, were generally worse at her menstrual periods. Physical examination revealed no evidence of cardiac disease, nor did special investigations confirm a physician's expressed suspicions of "ovarian trouble or possible thyroid toxicity." However, the psychiatric history showed that while the symptoms had no relationship to exertion or other physical stresses, they very definitely depended on certain situational factors.

After her husband's departure, the patient had resumed her former work as the private secretary of a minor industrial executive, with whom she had had occasional sexual relations before her marriage. Her employer attempted to renew their liaison, but out of loyalty to her husband (and also because of jealousy over her employer's other affairs) the patient had resisted; nevertheless, being sexually passionate and deprived, she was erotically aroused by his advances and sometimes responded to them just short of intercourse. The patient first experienced her anxiety symptoms in connection with such episodes; later they began to occur when she was not conscious of so direct a relationship, e.g., on her way to work, at USO dances, or while witnessing war movies that intensified her reactive guilt. The exacerbation of her anxiety during menstruation was similarly related to heightened erotic cravings during this period and was also manifested by frankly sexual dreams and fantasies.

## CASE 4 Ancillary Use of Amytal To Confirm Relevant Data

A forty-year-old engineer, while away from his wife for several months on a professional assignment, had an intensive extramarital affair and returned home contrite and guilt-ridden. Soon afterward, he was informed by a jealous neighbor that his wife had been seen in the company of other men in suspicious circumstances. In overcompensatory anger, he challenged her to give a complete accounting of herself, which she did, in full truthfulness denying any unfaithfulness. Unfortunately, however, in covert retaliation she also insisted on telling him "the whole truth" about herself once and for all and, therefore, described two casual premarital affairs that had occurred long before she had met her husband. This succeeded in driving him into a state of agitation and near collapse in which not only his marriage but also his business and social status were seriously threatened.

After the second interview the patient began to see that what he dreaded was not his wife's unfaithfulness, but the collapse of a system of fantasied personal primacy that had begun with his parent's indulgence, his own unusual success in school, and later dominance of his familial and social group. As these fantasies were put in a more realistic setting, his severe depression was mitigated and a crisis in his affairs thus averted. However, one crucial issue remained: Since his wife, in claiming virginity at the time of their marriage, had lied to him, could she now also be lying after all? Could he have *no* further trust in her or anyone else?

It is possible that in this case protracted therapy could have resolved this rationalization and much else that it represented; meanwhile, however, the patient's professional mobility and financial affairs would have suffered, and, worse, his wife and children would have been in a prolonged state of stress and insecurity. The therapist had interviewed the wife and was convinced that she had been faithful and truthful, but he also knew that if he insisted that the husband accept this as an established fact, he would verbally assent but actually continue to doubt. An alternative plan was therefore proposed and agreed to by all concerned: The wife would be given an intravenous injection of Sodium Amytal, a drug that purportedly diminished communicative inhibitions, in the husband's presence; moreover, the patient would be permitted to question her directly in any way he desired—*provided that he agreed not to continue to doubt the veracity of whatever she said.*

The technique was successful. Under Amytal, the wife repeated substantially what she had stated before and in a most convincing fashion. Because by now the patient wanted desperately to believe her, he did so, and he felt another foundation-stone under his citadel of security put back in place. Only two more interviews were necessary; twelve years later he and his wife were still attributing—somewhat inaccurately—his complete recovery and their reunion to the trial of the Amytal administration.

## Phobic–Obsessive–Compulsive Syndromes

These are characterized by persistent thoughts, fantasies, and fears (*obsessions*) that, although recognized by the patient himself as partly irrational, nevertheless lead to rigidly patterned modes of behavior. Typically also, when these *compulsions* are frustrated or interfered with, he reacts with intense anxiety as described. In such cases the patient may have developed an ardent routine of prejudices, avoidances, and rituals and may resent any change in these as fiercely as he would a challenge to his religion. Inquiry may therefore readily reveal the nature of his neurotic difficulties, but therapy may be covertly resented.

CASE 5 Phobic–Compulsive Stuttering

A male patient complained that he experienced marked

anxiety and stuttered almost unintelligibly whenever he had to give an impromptu verbal report of his work to his supervisor or to a meeting of co-workers; conversely, no matter how well he had memorized his remarks, he experienced much less difficulty if he could read them from a previously prepared manuscript. Investigation showed that he worked under conditions of intense rivalry and distrust, that spontaneous verbal exchanges with his colleagues entailed the more or less conscious danger that the patient might let slip expressions of contempt or anger, and that under such circumstances his speech became compulsively stilted, hesitant, and inhibited to the point of stuttering. In contrast, he could read safely from a manuscript, if the latter were meticulously prepared and carefully censored beforehand.

## CASE 6 Phobic Reactions

An eighteen-year-old girl was brought to the psychiatric outpatient clinic by her family, who stated that they were greatly concerned over the patient's irrational fear of small pets: dogs, cats, even canaries. So marked was the patient's apprehensiveness in this regard that, to guard against the possibility that such an animal might somehow enter the house at night, she insisted on locking all the doors and windows in the house and those of her own and her parents' bedrooms, while leaving an intercommunicating door between the two rooms open. Psychiatric examination revealed many other obsessions, compulsions, and neurotic symptoms, but the origin of the animal phobia was of particular interest.

### HISTORY

The patient had been a particularly indulged child until about the age of four, but she had then been almost completely displaced in her parents' affections when her mother gave birth to a long-anticipated son. The patient at first showed frank jealousy of her infant brother. When this merely increased what she sensed to be her parents' rejection of her, she became an apparently devoted sister except for one significant displacement: She was persistently destructive of her brother's clothes and other belongings, and particularly so of his mechanically animated toys. The parents, distressed by the patient's behavior but blind to its motivations, sought to change it by giving her a puppy, in order, as they remembered it, "to show Anne how cute and lovable any pet could be." Anne professed delight and seemed to cherish the pet; once, however, in her parents' absence, she so mistreated it that they later found it dead. Her punishment, reinforced by an intuitive recognition by the parents of the unconscious intent of the patient's act, was unusually severe. The patient's overt hostilities and destructiveness diminished; unfortunately, she developed various other neurotic patterns, prominent among which were a recurrent anxiety syndrome and a persistent fear of being alone with small animals of any description. Now thoroughly alarmed, the parents again began to shower attentions on the patient but, regrettably, mainly on the rationalized basis that she was a "sick, nervous child" who needed frequent medical and pediatric consultations. As may have been expected, this merely fixated the patient's phobias and other neurotic reactions until, after many years of well-meaning parental and medical mismanagement, she was referred for psychiatric therapy.

## Depressive Syndromes

Typical symptoms include absence of appetite (*anorexia,* sometimes alternating with *bulimia,* impulsive eating), variable constipation, insomnia or troubled sleep, loss of weight, easy fatigability, hypochondriacal preoccupations, sexual impotence or frigidity, subjective complaints of inability to concentrate, and feelings of failure, guilt, and hopelessness with, in severe cases, melancholy ruminations about death and suicide. Intermittent periods of forced, hollow cheerfulness and restless, distracted overactivity (*hypomania*) may occur, but are almost invariably succeeded by even deeper depressive reactions. A patient who expands his complaints along these lines is expressing a desperate need for concern and assistance, and, if these are not furnished, he may suffer or die (by suicide) as surely as one not given aid for a failing heart. Most moderate depressions, fortunately, respond to mild sedatives, a protective milieu, and friendly supportive therapeutic relationships that tide the patient over critical periods and prevent tragic consequences.

CASE 7 Depressive Reaction

A twenty-two-year-old girl was brought to the university clinics with the history that for the preceding three months she had suffered from symptoms characteristic of a severe depression: insomnia, marked anorexia, loss of weight, despondency, fatigue, obsessive preoccupations with the possibility that somehow she had been maritally unfaithful, and recurrent ideas of suicide. The patient's account of her present illness indicated that, against her family's active opposition, she had contracted a romantic but hasty marriage to a naval petty officer, who proved to be a suspicious, hyper-emotional individual, and that their marital life had been stormy and traumatic for the few weeks before he was sent overseas. The patient was highly disturbed by his departure and became more so when, shortly afterward, a medical examination revealed that she was pregnant and syphilitic. Frantic letters to her husband remained unanswered, and the patient, feeling abandoned and betrayed by everyone in her acute distress, reacted with the severe depression noted above. Her past history, however, revealed that she had been a healthy, active, normal child and that she had made good scholastic and social adjustments throughout her develop-mental years and in her university work, after which she had held responsible positions as an executive assistant until her marriage. Specific inquiry disclosed only relatively minor neurotic or depressive reactions to previous frustrations and disappointments, including the death of her idolized father and the subsequent loss of her family's fortune. In fact, she had been remarkably versatile and stable until her ill-starred wartime marriage and its succession of adversities had precipitated her presenting illness. Despite its evident severity, therefore, a good prognosis was given, and treatment was directed along realistic lines.

COURSE

The patient was hospitalized for protection and nursing care, the odium of the syphilis was removed, insofar as pos-sible, by factual reassurances, adequate therapy was instituted, and a family reunion was arranged by multiple interviews in which reconciliation was made to appear desirable all around.

Similarly, with the cooperation of military and Red Cross authorities, the patient's husband was located and tactfully informed of the situation. He promptly wrote her that he had not been in a position to receive her letters previously, but that he was devoted to her and was sure the child was his; moreover, he admitted that she had contracted the syphilis from him. Within three weeks the patient had recovered her health, spirits, and self-reliance and was back at full-time work. She delivered the child without physical or psychiatric complications and continued to show normal readjustments in nearly every sphere of behavior during a three-year follow-up.

## Pharmacotoxic States

In these days of continuous concern, compounded by cacophonous commercials ceaselessly commending a multiplicity of nepenthic notions, lotions, and potions, it has also become necessary to inquire skillfully as to the nostrums with which our troubled patient has been dosing himself. As a complication of other rationalized escapisms, excessive consumption of alcohol, with its hangovers of headache, residual tremors, irritable lassitude, and impaired cerebration, is an old story. However, the patient may also have been taking excessive quantities of sedatives, tranquilizers, or stimulants, with resultant episodes of partial disorientation, sensory disturbances, confusion of thought and imagery, and clouded memories of disinhibited sexual and aggressive behavior. Conversely, sudden discontinuations or changes in his drug intake may have occasioned various sensory disturbances, muscular spasms, gastrointestinal dysfunctions, vague physiologic cravings, and other *withdrawal symptoms*. Especially in teen-age patients, inquiries must be made as to the secret smoking of "pot" or "grass" (marijuana), the inhalation of volatile intoxicants (e.g., toluene or other commercial solvents in paints or adhesives), the consumption of "downers" (barbiturates) or "uppers" (amphetamines), or even more dangerous individual or group experiments with lysergic acid (LSD), mescaline, and other delirium-producing *psychotomimetic* substances. Irresponsible or naïve parents may use the encompassing euphemism "nervousness" as a cover for destructive, perverse, delinquent, or even semihallucinatory behavior in their intoxicated offspring and may try to obtain yet more "tranquilizers" for their "nervous" youngsters. Obviously, in such cases, a different diagnosis is essential for proper therapy: the discontinuation of harmful drug intake, the control of withdrawal symptoms, and the correction of the rebellious and escapist behavior of which the patient's addiction to drugs may be but one manifestation.

### CASE 8 Psychophysiologic Skin Reaction—Neurodermatitis with Barbiturate Intoxication

A psychiatric consultation was requested for a twenty-five-year-old married woman who had been admitted to the dermatological service with complaints of a chronic itching (pruritic) eczema, complicated by an overlying dermatitis that had appeared after she had begun to take large quantities of "nerve medicine" two months previously. On examination, the patient was found to be stuporous, disorientated, and vaguely hallucinated; bromism was suspected and confirmed by two blood bromide readings of 215 and 205 mg. per 100 cc.

The patient was transferred to the psychiatric service where, after several days of forced saline fluids and suspension of all other medication, her confusion and mild ataxia abated, the papular rash began to clear, and communication could be established.

#### HISTORY

She was an only child of parents who persisted in being theatrical in every sense of the word and who lived an erratic, footloose life of travel, mutual recriminations, separations, passionate reunions, and histrionic scenes at home and in public. Left to herself, the patient had grown to take great pride in her slim, graceful body, had cultivated it with much training and exercise, and had delighted in displaying as much of it as permissible as a professional dancer. Sexually, she had been promiscuous, mainly because of the narcissistic satisfaction she experienced in having herself fondled. In contrast, intercourse itself was an anticlimax, and the patient was orgasmiscally frigid. After many conquests, she had married a well-to-do man who professed deathless infatuation with her and who promised her complete financial security, freedom from the usual marital obligations, and an untrammeled pursuit of her "career." Unfortunately, these supposed advantages had not materialized; worse, despite every contraceptive precaution, she became pregnant. The patient remembered the repugnance with which she watched her skin become blotchy and her breasts and abdomen enlarge, and her anguish at the thought that "maybe I'll lose my shape and beauty." Early in pregnancy general pruritis appeared, and the patient began to rub and, finally, to scratch herself with imperfectly repressed thoughts of attacking her child through her own body. Her husband, however, would not agree to an abortion and, sensing his wife's continued rejection of the child after it was born, insisted that his mother come to live with them to care for it. Friction between the two women ensued immediately, and the patient's dermatitis became worse. In this connection, she remembered that for the first time she began to experience an almost masturbatory element in her pruritis; her scratching would reach an orgasmic intensity followed by a form of detumescence and relief. The patient consulted various dermatologists who prescribed baths, lotions, and salves, supplemented after the birth of her child by sedative prescriptions containing bromides and Luminal for her "nervousness." These had finally caused the complicating toxic rash and delirium for which she was admitted to the hospital.

COURSE UNDER THERAPY

With the cessation of bromide and barbiturate medication and the administration of sodium chloride solution, the patient's sensorium cleared, and her drug rash gradually disappeared. As is often the case in narcissistically introspective persons, a working insight was not difficult to establish; a far greater problem was to find an acceptable field of expression for attitudes that were scarcely less modifiable for being made explicit. A compromise was finally worked out: A relatively devoted governess acceptable to both the patient and her husband replaced the mother-in-law in caring for the child. The husband was made more cooperative in the arrangement by the tactful implication that, as he himself had realized before his marriage, he could not force his wife into motherly duties. Should he perisist in trying, she might once again, quite unconsciously, try to punish him by impairing the beauty he still greatly admired. For her part, the patient also compromised: She applied for and won the part of a frustrated career woman in a television soap opera. Thus, while remaining with her husband and child in the public role of a devoted wife and mother, she had a daily opportunity to identify with her theatrical parents in a fervor of broadcast emotion that won her specialized audience's acclaim and her sponsor's financial gratitude. In a five-year follow-up, she reported that no further pregnancies, rashes, or deliria had occurred and that she was quite happy in what she termed her creativity as a "television artist."

## Psychoses

These are indicated when the patient's relationships to the therapist are grossly deviant, his thoughts illogical, bizarre, or hallucinatory, the concomitant affects manifestly inappropriate, and the experiences he relates indicative of delusions of persecution, grandeur, or uncontrolled and possibly dangerous impulsivity. Just as it would be the physician's duty in the case of a reportable disease, it is here again the therapist's obligation to protect the patient and others by alerting his family and friends and by taking every measure—including legal steps if indicated—to see that appropriate consultation and protection are available or institutional care arranged for if necessary.

CASE 9 Melancholia

An intelligent, but physically rather unattractive, Catholic schoolteacher married secretly at the age of thirty-eight and a year later became pregnant. Her husband, an improvident, middle-aged ne'er-do-well, did not like the prospect of the patient's losing her position if her marriage were discovered. He therefore strongly urged her to have an abortion; when she refused, he deserted her. This left the patient no alternative but to violate her religious scruples and attempt to abort herself, not only to keep her job and social position, but to remove all memories of her unhappy marital experience.

Her crude attempts failed and the patient was forced to reveal the date and fate of her marriage to her family. On their advice—tinged with considerable covert condemnation—she obtained a leave of absence from her job and reversed her conscious attitude toward her pregnancy; in fact, she began to plan with ominously overcompensatory zeal for every detail of the immediate and remote future of her child, on whom she intended to focus her "every remaining interest in life." She was delivered normally at term but, again tragically, the child was congenitally deformed and died within a few hours. The patient almost immediately entered into a deep melancholic state in which she refused to eat, slept fitfully or not at all, lost twenty pounds in as many days, and needed mechanical restraint to prevent suicidal attempts. This acute phase gradually passed, but for months of institutionalization thereafter she had to be nursed, washed, dressed, spoon fed, and cared for as though she herself were a child. During this period she seemed to have lost all her former intellectual and social interests: She could not be induced to read, listen to news or music, or engage in occupational or group activities. After visits by her family she was particularly querulous and demanding; at other times she sat rocking and chanting to herself in an almost inaudible, repetitious sing-song in which the following content could sometimes be distinguished: She accused herself of having committed "the Unforgivable Sin," the nature of which she never further specified. The Catholic Church and all its clerical hierarchy had been informed of this. Indeed, the Holy Trinity Themselves had condemned her to eternal perdition, and this was a universal catastrophe, because she herself had become "Mrs. Pope Pius XIV." Even now her womb was "pregnant with a Holy Child," which had to be guarded and protected eternally. These bizarre and self-excoriative fantasies were charged with an intensity of affect difficult to describe, but usually sensed as deeply melancholic. Yet, despite her apparent suffering, the patient concentrated into her melancholia a wealth of adaptation that seemed psychologically essential if her lot was to be bearable at all. In confessional mode, the patient condemned herself as a lost soul, automatically excommunicated from the Church because of her "unforgivable sin"—her attempt to murder an unborn child. At the same time she compensated for the guilt by the grandiose and subtly self-preserving fantasy that the entire Church was concerned with her particular conduct. Further, her punishment would be supervised by the Heavenly Court Itself, Who, in view of her exalted position as the "wife" of a future pontiff, might eventually condone her transgressions and grant them absolution. Similarly, while she confessed her previous wishes for the death of her un- wanted baby, she overcompensated for these by a delusion of possessing a deathless child forever reincorporated into her womb. Finally, in her external behavior she made herself actually a helpless being who required all the care and pro- tection of a newborn infant in the midst of a loving and forgiving hospital family.

## Neurologic Disorders

Among the less frequent connotations of the patient's symptoms are other conditions to which the diagnostician must remain alert:

### PSYCHOMOTOR EPILEPSY OR ITS EQUIVALENTS

These comprise momentary suspensions of consciousness (*absences*) or confusional–amnesic states with or without localized muscular (*Jacksonian*) twitches or transient "automatic" behavior (*fugues*), often followed by fatigue and headache. If the diagnosis is con- firmed by direct observation supplemented by pathognomonic wave-forms on tracings of cerebral voltage (*electroencephalograms*), these episodes may be at least partially controlled by drugs such as phenobarbital, Dilantin, or Phenurone; or, if persistent, in some cases by an operation on the cerebral cortex (*temporal lobotomy*).

### CASE 10 Posttraumatic Epilepsy with Character Regression

The patient, a twenty-seven-year-old unmarried woman, was admitted with complaints of major convulsive (*gran mal*) seizures and progressive deterioration of behavior to the point of occupational and social incompetence.

The initial week of the patient's stay in the hospital was devoted to a careful physical and neurological reexamination as to a possible organic basis for her seizures. Aside from a congenital facial disfigurement, the findings were nondeterminative, and recheck air and electroencephalograms also revealed no definite evidences of a focal lesion for her attacks. On one occasion, when a seizure was observed in its entirety, the following occurred: The patient seemingly had no warning of the onset of the attack, the first indications of which were a blank expression, followed within a few seconds by clonic spasms in her left arm, ending in a cramped position of the hand. Clonic spasms then spread to her shoulders, face, and right arm, and these were soon followed by slow clonic contractions of her right face and arm. The patient remained seated throughout the seizure, which persisted for about five minutes. There was no incontinence, nor did the spasms spread to the lower extremities. She remained confused and somewhat ataxic for ten minutes and afterward claimed complete amnesia for the entire episode. Moreover, there were no residual headaches, feelings of weakness, or sensations of depersonalization.

In psychiatric interviews it was determined that even before the onset of her epilepsy (which the patient attributed to a head trauma in a fall twelve years previously) she had always been an insecure, emotionally unstable individual, inclined to overreact with excessive ambitiousness, restless activity, and a demanding attitude toward her family and associates. This had been reflected in her later life history as an inability to establish lasting friendships, to contract a stable marriage, or to work out rational plans in occupational or other spheres. The patient had also been emotionally overattached to her father, whose favorite she had considered herself to be. At his death, soon after her accident, she entered into a prolonged depression characterized by guilt feelings that she had contributed to his demise by her irresponsibility, drinking, and finally her physical "repulsiveness." The patient continued to work fairly steadily, but her efficiency was impaired not only by her seizures but also by her truculence, impatience, and affective instability. These had increased to the point at which, during the three years preceding her admission, she had not been able to maintain steady work; on the contrary, she had become almost completely dependent on her two sisters and lived with one of them. This dependence was accompanied by overt signs of deterioration and regression, so that she became careless in her clothes, isolated in her social adjustments, and actually resistant to treatment in that she refused to take the medication prescribed for her attacks.

The patient's therapy, on the physical side, consisted in medication designed to diminish the frequency and severity of her seizures. For this purpose Dilantin was administered up to 0.3 gm. daily with the addition of phenobarbital 0.09 gm. at bedtime. Special emphasis, however, was also laid on the necessity for accepting her seizures as being partly inevitable and on her adjusting to them in a more adequate manner. The same attitude was urged on the patient's family, who were then led to see that the patient's regressive tendencies must be counteracted by encouraging her to adopt occupational and social adjustments. With the aid of a social worker, the following plans were made for the patient's extra-mural readjustments:

1.  She was to take a job as file clerk, since one was immediately available. If this position did not work out satisfactorily, other possibilities, such as private secretarial work, home typing, etc., were to be explored.
2.  She was to remain with the older married sister only until more emancipated living arrangements were possible. (This was particularly necessary inasmuch as the sister was beginning to become highly irritated by the patient and had begun to show her hostility in various overt ways.)
3.  Various recreational and social outlets were to be recultivated by the patient with the aid and encouragement of the family and the social worker.
4.  The patient was to remain on the present Dilantin and phenobarbital dosage.
5.  She was given instructions as to a mildly ketogenic diet, the avoidance of overeating or the intake of excessive fluids, and the methods of handling situations in which epileptic seizures might be dangerous.
6.  She was to return to the out-patient department regularly for further instructions.

The family, in separate interviews, was given more understanding of both the idiopathic and personal elements in the patient's illness and thereafter seemed to be more cooperative.

Unfortunately, the patient, in line with her past regression, her inertia, and the secondary gain she had derived from her illness, at first adopted the attitude that it was up to her physician to "cure her" of her attacks before she could actively participate in any plans for her occupational, social, and other readjustments. Later, however, she accepted the necessity of such adjustment, expressed her gratitude, and continued her cooperation in extramural rehabilitation.

OTHER ORGANIC IMPAIRMENTS OF CEREBRAL FUNCTION

These may range etiologically from the aftereffects of central nervous system infections through damages from concussion, hemorrhage, embolism, or tumors, to the ravages of old age. Predictably, many patients who suspect grave and progressive impairments of their physical and intellectual powers will try to conceal or minimize serious symptoms such as localized headaches, visual and auditory impairment, recurrent fainting, and even convulsive episodes and dismiss them all as "just being overworked and a bit nervous now and then—all I really need is a nerve pill and a tonic." However, inquiry will reveal unmistakably progressive impairment of intellectual capacities and motor skills, loss of memory for recent events, and disintegration of personal and social habits. Nevertheless, even when neurological, ophthalmic, auditory, cerebrospinal fluid, and x-ray findings confirm the diagnosis of focal or generalized cerebral lesions, the patient is still a human being who will, all the more, need reassurance, easing of strains and obligations, and guidance in utilizing his remaining capacities.

CASE 11 Alzheimer's Disease with Additional Psychophysical Dysfunction—Amytal as an Aid in Differential Diagnoses

A forty-one-year-old married woman was brought to the university hospital because, according to the family, she had become progressively more forgetful, slovenly, confused, and irritable during the previous three years, and more recently, almost uncontrollably quarrelsome and aggressive. Neurologic examination revealed bilateral rapid nystagmoid movements. pallor of the temporal portions of both optic disks, and positive Hoffman reflexes. The mental status, moreover, showed signs indicative of organic cortical aphasia: The patient had difficulty in expressing herself and contorted her features while seeking for what she wanted to say. She was confused as to the time and sequence of past events. She answered "Yes" or "Fine" to evade misunderstood, though simple, questions and followed her statements with a doubtful "Is that right?" or the stereotyped phrase "Hold the phone." She frequently stated, "There is something in my head that does not allow things to come through clearly." Her memory was deficient in all spheres, as were her replies to simple tests of calculation, association, orientation, and general information. Whenever an attempt was made to obtain some account of her illness, she replied with "You can worm these things out of me. Go on asking questions."

A week after her admission, she was given 0.3 gm. of Sodium Amytal intravenously. The record of her reactions is as follows: She at first became combative, talked rapidly, tried to pull the stethoscope from the examiner and became restless. However, she also grew talkative and during the next half hour gave a connected account of her life. This was remarkably clear and detailed and dealt frankly with early family and school experiences, occupational adjustments, various love affairs previous to her marriage and sexual and economic dissatisfactions thereafter. Next she discussed what she thought was the precipitating cause of her illness: "overwork and aggravation," with final physical exhaustion from having devoted the last three years of her life to taking care of her blind and aged mother and trying to run the family business. While under the effects of the Amytal, she spoke rapidly and surely and without the pseudoaphasic difficulties that had characterized her expressions at all previous interviews. When the effects of the drug had worn off, however, the patient resumed her previous mannerisms, taciturnity, and uncooperativeness.

It was evident that the patient suffered from an organic cerebral disease called an Alzheimer syndrome but that superadded to her neurological defects were disabilities arising from functional depression and withdrawal. This was confirmed when the latter reactions were favorably influenced by two more Amytal interviews with appropriate follow-up psychotherapy.

# Psychiatric Therapies

## Therapeutic Preview

The foregoing diagnostic procedures should lead to the following measures:

### RELIEF OF SYMPTOMS

The patient's discomforts are first to be alleviated by every available means, including, when indicated, surgical consultation for conditions such as peptic ulcer or spastic colitis that originally may have been "functional" but have now become complicated by persistent organic lesions. However, opiates must be avoided, and sedatives, ataractic, and hypnotic drugs used with caution and changed or discontinued frequently to preclude addiction. When the patient's symptoms have abated sufficiently to render him more comfortable, mobile, and cooperative, every effort must be made to reevoke his initiative, to recultivate his neglected interests, skills, and activities, and thus to regain the confidence and self-respect that come only from useful accomplishment.

## SOCIAL REHABILITATION

Later, the therapist will use gentle reasoning and personal guidance to induce the patient to review his past misconceptions and animosities, abandon childlike patterns of behavior that have long since lost their effectiveness, revise his goals and values, and adopt a more realistic and rewarding ("mature") style of life. To aid in this reorientation, the enlightened cooperation of the patient's family, friends, employer, and others may, with the patient's assent, be secured and fully utilized to strengthen his personal and communal securities—a *sine qua non* in relieving his social anxieties and their manifold expressions in deviant behavior.

## REESTABLISHMENT OF INNER SECURITIES

Finally, the patient's personal faiths, instead of being depreciated or undermined, should be respected or supplemented so as to furnish him with what all of us require as fundamentally as we do our strength and our friends: a belief in life's purpose, meaning, and value. In this sense, medicine as a humanitarian science can never be in conflict with philosophy or religion. All three seem to have been designed by a beneficent providence to preserve, console, and comfort man.

## CASE 12  Therapy of Anxiety–Phobic Reactions with Transient Motor Dysfunction—Military Implications

A twenty-eight-year-old man complained that since his service in the navy two years previously, he had suffered from episodes of anxiety described as "a stifling in the heart and in my breath and a feeling of being all tensed up and in a cold sweat. I get scared and want to run away from I don't know what." The episodes almost invariably occurred when he heard a loud, unexpected noise, when he was forced to ride upward in a crowded elevator, when he had to wait his turn in a line of people, or when he saw a motion picture depicting military maneuvers. He had built up various protective patterns such as avoiding crowds and theaters, walking upstairs when- ever he could, insisting on absolute quiet at home, or even wearing cotton in his ears; but these devices on the whole had been ineffectual, and his attacks of acute anxiety had continued to be frequent and severe. Moreover, his sleep was increasingly disturbed by a repetitive dream in which he tried desperately to reach the head of a column of people, always failed, and inevitably woke in a state of deep apprehension.

PHYSICAL AND LABORATORY FINDINGS

These were normal, and special examinations showed no evidences of neurologic or endocrine disease with one excep- tion: The basal metabolic rate was reported as moderately high.

PAST HISTORY

The patient indicated that he had led a somewhat sheltered life but had made consistent educational and vocational progress and he had become a trusted executive in an insurance firm. He had married happily and had shown no overt neurotic symptoms until the onset of his presenting complaints.

PRESENT ILLNESS

At first the patient was vague and evasive as to the cir- cumstances of onset, but after several interviews he finally began to trace many of his difficulties to his experiences during naval training. Significantly, he began by recalling only defensive "screen memories" in which the navy, and not he, was made to appear at fault. As an "economically minded citizen," he had been "outraged" by what he saw of extrava- gant navy practices: tossing soiled dishes or blankets over- board instead of washing them, reckless waste of food, etc. Gradually, however, as his own guilts became more evident and his anxieties over them more acceptable, significant facts emerged.

In 1942 when the patient was drafted, he had chosen the

navy because its training ground was close to his home. He had become unstable and occasionally dejected during the interminable irrational routines of "boot training" but had held up fairly well until he was sent from his base camp, assigned to duty in the magazine deck of a destroyer, and placed in a crowded team of men organized to pass ammunition through a mechanical elevator to the gun crews. He experienced considerable fear on initial contact with the imminent dangers of actual warfare, and it was noted that he was always the first to take his assigned place in line at drills for "evacuate post" or "abandon ship." However, he was able to find two sources of security: the generally high morale of the ship, and a feeling of personal safety and pride in the smooth efficiency of his ammunition squad. One day, however, one of the most skillful members of his team dropped a live shell on the deck—a harmless occurrence in itself, but one that represented to the patient the possibility of a magazine explosion that would mean certain death. The next day he noted a peculiar stiffness in his right arm and shoulder that interfered increasingly with his work of lifting shells from an ammunition rack to the elevator—a sensorimotor symptom that, apparently, was a neurotic compromise between self-preservative fears and a sense of duty and devotion to his job. The medical officer, noting the muscular tension and the limitations of joint motion in the patient's arms, suspected arthritis and sent the patient to sick bay. Here, two days later, the second and final trauma occurred: The patient heard that a serious explosion in the magazine of another ship in the harbor had killed eight men. His anxiety attacks immediately became more intense and frequent; his nights were tense and sleepless; and he became so susceptible to startle reactions in response to sudden noises or flashes of light that the neurotic nature of his illness was easily recognized. Unfortunately, no therapy was instituted, and the patient was given a medical discharge. He returned home, where his arm rapidly improved; nevertheless, his anxiety attacks and his symbolic fears of crowds, elevators, and war scenes continued almost unabated. One other episode may be mentioned as illustrative of the semantic spread of these symbolisms: When he returned to work, his employer welcomed him but explained that, since his old associates had been promoted during the wartime expansion of the company, the patient "would have to take his place in line" for his turn at advancement. Although this was what the patient had expected, the phrase "place in line" induced a severe attack of anxiety, followed by uncontrolled sobbing. Similar reactions of anxiety and emotional instability seriously interfered with his occupational and social readjustments and eventually occasioned his admission to the clinics.

THERAPY

In brief, this consisted in hospitalization for temporary removal from current stresses and responsibilities, sedation to control insomnia and general tension, and a complete diagnostic check-up to allay the patient's half-wishful "fears" that he was suffering from some serious physical disease, instead of a humiliating "nervous breakdown." When adequate rapport had been gained, the nature of the patient's conflicts and his various symbolic defenses against pervasive anxiety were traced to his military experiences, and preliminary "intellectual" insight was thus established. Concurrently, he was reintroduced into increasingly active and competitive group activities such as card-playing, quoits, and baseball. In this way, too, he was induced by the therapist to enter situations he had previously avoided: a casual ride down on the elevator to the playground, passage through the noisy hospital basement, the interpolation of a previously disturbing newsreel shown at an evening's movie show, and so on. Recurrences of mild anxiety during each such experience were interpreted simply and directly in preparation for the next and possibly more difficult one; in this manner the patient's phobic tendencies were both anticipated and eliminated through preparatory set and subsequent mastery in action.

CHANGE IN BASAL METABOLIC RATE

This also showed an interesting reversal: A second test given three weeks after the first indicated a metabolic rate of plus 3. Inquiry at this time revealed the cause of the discrepancy in the two BMR readings. The patient recollected that when the mask of the apparatus was fitted to his face for the first time, he had vaguely associated it with a memory of seeing oxygen administered to seriously injured war casualties, and had experienced severe anxiety that, with some difficulty, he had concealed from the technician at the time. On the second test this reaction was minimal, with a normal metabolic reading as a result.

A few days later the patient left the hospital greatly improved, returned to work, and has since remained symptom-free except for mild startle reactions when exposed to unexpectedly intense sensory stimuli.

The case presents certain almost obvious but hightly instructive features. Most prominent is the development of an unconsciously determined motor dysfunction (the arm paralysis) as a temporary adjustment to an otherwise insoluble motivational conflict between need for participation in a group defense (duty) and fear of personal danger. The paralysis temporarily resolved the impasse and provided some escape. However, the patient's fears were again exacerbated by the harbor explosion, and there was a spread of phobic aversions to various "objective" and "verbal" symbols—noises, elevators, crowds, people in line. All such associations reactivated the conflict and again provoked intense reactions. Fortunately, the patient was able to reexplore his anxieties under the guidance of a therapist he had learned to trust. Thus he was able to reorient his symbolizations, desensitize his reactions, rearrange his patterns of living, and recover his faith in their values. Nevertheless, the case illustrates some of the residual effects of war neurosis that will affect countless thousands of men long after their acute traumatic experiences are over and apparently "forgotten."

This case illustrates some of the general principles of therapy, but their application must take account of multiple clinical contingencies: the patient's constitutional predispositions, his age and sex, the type, intensity, and duration of his disorders, his economic, social, and cultural milieu, and many other factors. This complexity has led some practitioners to declare that "psychotherapy is an art rather than a science," but once again we can avoid sententious obscurity by the ever-useful semantic wisdom embodied in our language: Webster, for example, defines *art* as "skill derived from knowledge and experience."

# Behavior Disorders of Childhood

## INFANCY

In large part, "mental hygiene" at this time of life is preventive rather than curative and might well begin before the child is born. If the mother suffers dietary deficiencies during pregnancy (especially during the critical third to sixth month), or takes excessive doses of certain hormones, antibiotics, or sedatives, or is subjected to severe emotional shocks, the child she is carrying may be seriously and permanently injured. Birth should, of course, be expertly conducted to prevent infant asphyxia or prolonged compression of its skull, and aftercare must ensure respiration, asepsis, constant temperature, and special food for the neonate, especially if premature. There is no evidence that mother's milk is nutritionally superior to pediatric formulae. But if the infant is not breast-fed, it must in other ways be physically stimulated by rocking, fondling, and gentle play to promote its sensory and motor development and emotional responsiveness. In this respect, Anna Freud, John Bowlby, T. A. Bourne, and others, have demonstrated that children given adequate physical care in orphanages but deprived of individualized love and attention during the crucial first four years of life lose the capacity to form warm relationships and, instead, develop serious and persistent disturbances of behavior variously called *autism, protophrenia,* or *childhood schizophrenia.*

## EARLY METABOLIC DEFICIENCIES

On rare occasions, children are born with a congenital incapacity to metabolize certain sugars, fats, or other dietary elements such as the component amino acid phenylalanine. Unless these deficiencies are detected within the first few weeks and special diets prescribed, these substances or their metabolic byproducts accumulate in the body and permanently injure the brain and other organs. Fortunately, reliable tests are now available for such hidden defects and should be routinely used by obstetricians, pediatricians, and parents.

CONGENITAL ABNORMALITIES

The birth of a mongoloid child is due to a rare accident in the early divisions of the fertilized ovum and is no certain indication of an "hereditary taint" in either parent. Maldeveloped extremities, cleft palate, or other deformities are, of course, immediately apparent at birth, but it may take several weeks, months, or years to detect partial deafness, impaired vision, or susceptibility to epileptic convulsions. In any case, the extent of the handicap must be accurately assayed and objectively accepted; steps may then be taken to minimize its physical effects on the child's future. Each child presents a highly individualized problem, but the general principles of procedure are these:

1. If the infant is so seriously handicapped either physically (e.g., without functional arms or legs) or mentally (a general intelligence below half normal—i.e., optimum IQ less than 50) that adequate adjustments outside a private or public institution would be extremely difficult or impossible, then it is to the child's own and everyone else's advantage to arrange for prolonged hospitalization to develop its maximal potentials, or to accept permanent institutional care. Parental objections to the latter course on the basis of "devotion to our poor unfortunate darling" or "the advantages of loving care at home until it outgrows its handicap" require a sympathetic hearing but firm correction, since such pleas are usually based on threatened familial pride and attempts to deny reality rather than on objective considerations for the welfare of the handicapped child, its siblings, and its future associates.

2. If the child's capacities permit extramural adaptations, its future happiness may be promoted as follows:

PHYSICAL HANDICAPS

Crossed eyes can be corrected by glasses or by surgery before one becomes functionally useless. Congenitally malformed arms or legs can often be fitted with ingenious artificial prostheses that restore almost complete function—a very important consideration if the child is to have character-forming play and group experiences with peers who might otherwise reject and embitter him. By modern methods, even a deaf-mute can be taught to communicate, become literate, and perhaps develop unusual talents—witness the classic example of Helen Keller.

INTELLECTUAL RETARDATION

Children with a rating below about three-fourths normal on reliable intelligence tests (IQ below 75) should not be exposed to competition with other children at home or in standard schools, since they soon feel inadequate and alienated. They may then regress to infantile helplessness, retreat into self-isolation, or develop patterns of rebellion and delinquency. Instead, they must first be given patient parental preparation at home and then placed in special environments where their basic education and training in social skills can be paced more slowly and carefully. In rare but fortunate cases, special manual, linguistic, musical, or even mathematical potentials may be discovered and developed that will compensate for intellectual defects in other spheres.

*Marriage of Retardates.* It has been reliably estimated that over 85 percent of mental retardation in this country is nonhereditary and that if every person with an intelligence quotient below 80 were prevented from having children, there would be no appreciable decrease of mental deficiency in future generations. Mental retardates who have demonstrated economic competence and social responsibility therefore have every right to marry and have progeny unless, in specific cases, a geneticist finds adequate reasons to the contrary.

PRECOCITY AND GENIUS

A different set of problems is presented by this opposite extreme. If a child's unique intellectual, mechanical, artistic, or other capacities are not recognized early and given encouragement, expression, and approbation, he may become bored, frustrated, isolated, restless, contemptuous, and rebellious. Care must be taken, nevertheless, to keep his development physically and mentally rounded, else he too would miss the essentials of play and of peer and adult camaraderie that are indispenable to the development of social skills and allegiances.

### CHILDHOOD NEUROSES

Many children develop "perverse" feeding habits, "night terrors," bedwetting, school phobias, and other patterns of "problem behavior." In most cases, the child is reacting to familial insecurities arising from neglect, parental conflicts, excessive expectations, sibling rivalries, or other such threats to its essential dependencies. The child may also behave in ways to *invite* censure and physical "punishment"—not because it is "masochistic" (a dynamically paradoxical term)—but because only in this manner can the child evoke its parents' concern and attention. Frequently, when the latter refer the problem to a "counselor," they are merely trying to avoid responsibility for the adverse home environment and may further isolate and stigmatize the child. Under such circumstances, the parents themselves should undertake therapy for their own as well as for the child's sake. Meanwhile, even in severe and persistent disorders a skillful therapist can, by more adequately perceiving and temporarily fulfilling the child's needs, partially substitute for delinquent parents, promote healthier peer and adult relationships, develop the child's skills and intellectual interests, and thus improve its social conduct despite adverse familial circumstances.

## Psychoanalytic Concepts of Child Behavior

In his later revisions of what he termed his *metapsychology*, Sigmund Freud extended the connotations of the term *libido* from its original meaning (erotic urge) to include almost every other motivation: survival, "self-love," nutritive seekings, material possessiveness, reactive hostility, etc. Freud could thus attribute all human behavior to successive "libidinal phases" in childhood. Since pristine Freudian theory is still taken seriously in some quarters, these phases are outlined, with comments as to their conceptual modifications in relation to therapy.

### Neonatal "Narcissism"

During the first few days or weeks of life, the child, knowing nothing of the "outside" world, takes what Freud called *polymorphous perverse pleasure* only in its own bodily functions. Biodynamically, of course, even the neonate "knows" that air is for breathing and crying and milk for swallowing and digesting. Indeed, since all we can ever "know" of the "outside" world is through our interpretive perceptions and bodily functions, all subsequent intellectual pursuits or physical activities are "autistic" and the term *perverse* is merely a Freudian pejorative. In either case, it is of the utmost importance that every child be subjected to pleasant "external" stimuli to an optimal degree so that its private "body image" of an "outside" world be correspondingly acceptable, else it will withdraw its budding interests, exclude that world, and then be called "narcissistic," or "schizoid."

### "Oral" Phase

This follows recognition by the child of the mother's breast as a primary "external" source of sustenance and protected dependence with surrogate residues in patterns such as thumb-sucking or caressing, kissing, and other symbolic components of adult erotic practices. A child deprived of actual or substitutive "oral gratifications" may be defensively resentful enough to refuse food or become reactively "grasping" and "incisive" (biting objects to hold them, as in premature weaning) and thus develop a compulsion to acquire and retain possessions throughout life. Therapy in childhood consists of providing not only more frequent feedings (as in a *demand schedule*) but more tender and reassuring mothering; later in life, residues of early frustrations may require considerable correction before social trusts and securities can be reestablished.

## "ANAL" PHASE

Eventually, however, every child must learn to accommodate to the customs and demands of his culture, and this becomes undeniably critical at the onset of bowel training. The child may react to this threat to his previous preeminence first by rebellion (continued soiling, destructiveness, tantrums, etc.) and later by a seeming over-compliance (excessive "cleanliness" and rigidly ritualistic habits leading to adult phobic–obsessive–compulsive behavior), which may be equally, though more covertly, punitive to the child's family and its later associates. Therapy is based on helping the child by ex-planation and example—and the adult by more complex com-munications—to learn that most forms of social compliance are no more a sacrifice of cherished omnipotence (though this is a precious illusion that cannot be directly attacked) than opening a door instead of trying to go directly through a wall is a sacrifice of efficiency, or stopping at a traffic light is being subservient. On the contrary, civilization epitomizes the rational concept that voluntary cultural adaptations are to the individual's advantage, and constitute a foundation upon which to build his personal power and creativity.

## "PHALLIC" PHASE

Freud believed that between the ages of four and six the child's *libido,* previously *cathected* to oral and anal functions, becomes concentrated on its genital organs, with the mother as the first sexual object. The little boy, therefore, wants to eliminate his father and possess his mother (the so-called *Oedipus complex*[1]), whereas the little girl wishes she, too, had a phallus (*penis envy*) with which to displace the father in her mother's affections. In this manner, *ambivalent* mixtures of dependent attachments and resentful hostili-ties toward the parents developed during earlier phases are further

---

[1] The term *complex* was adapted from the writings of Carl Jung, who held that all human conduct was complexly determined by prehistoric and cul-tural as well as individual genetic and experiential influences.

complicated by sexual jealousies and fears of specific physical punishment by the omnipotent father (*castration complex*). Therapy thereby becomes more involved, since the adult patient will unconsciously *transfer* to the therapist the disturbingly paradoxical attitudes of seductive reliance versus suspicion and distrust developed in early familial experiences, thus complicating the therapeutic relationship by a *transference neurosis*. The objectives of the analysis would then be to help the child or the unemancipated (*fixated*) adult to acquire *insight* into the origin and spurious nature of these *nuclear conflicts*, and to *mature:* expand his interests, goals, and attachments from the constricted circle of his childhood to the spheres of adult endeavor and attainment, peer friendships, and normal sexual, social, and cultural freedoms.

At this point, it may be helpful to point out that the Greek myths of Narcissus, Electra, Oedipus, *et al.* have much richer connotations than the simplistic interpretations attached to them in classical psychoanalytic metapsychology. For example, was Narcissus "in love with himself," as Freud implies in the term *narcissism*, or did he become so enamored of his vaguely reflected and wishfully idealized *image* that he forsook his friend Almeinas and his mistress Echo? Again, whether, as Eugene O'Neill would have it, mourning became Electra, it certainly became fatal to her mother Clytemnestra, her mother's lover Aegisthos, nearly so for her brother Orestes, and to practically everyone else involved. But far beyond these, perhaps the most inclusive and poignant of man's perennial vicissitudes are dramatized in Sophicles' trilogy on Oedipus—a succession of legends that, instead of epitomizing merely a middle-class Viennese son's supposed desires for coitus with his mother countered by Freudian fear of his father's terrible swift sword, deal much more deeply with nearly all human travail and triumph from infantile survival to the ultimate denial of death. Thus:

Laius, King of Thebes, is warned by an oracle that his son would slay him—as, indeed, all children will inevitably displace their elders. Torn by doubt and fear, Laius avoids the onus of infanticide and instead hobbles his child (as symbolically we tend to do) by pinning together the ankles of the newborn Oedipus (Greek: swollen feet) and—there being no Nilotic bulrushes about—leaves him in a basket on Mount Cathaeron. Like Moses, Oedipus is found by a kindly servant and adopted by Polybus, King of Corinth—as many of our own rejected children are partially rescued by baby-sitters, nursery teachers, pedagogues, and other parent surrogates. But Oedipus is never certain that he is "really" the true Prince of Corinth, cannot get satisfactory assurances from King Polybus or Queen Merope (who *can* be absolutely certain of his paternity?), and is further perplexed when he learns at Delphi that he is destined to kill his father and marry his mother. Trying to escape his fate (as who does not?), he vows never to see his putative parents Polybus or Merope again, and leaves Corinth to wander in search of what Erik Erikson would call his "true identity." At a crossroads outside Thebes, an old man disputes his right-of-way and is killed in the ensuing battle—as all oldsters who dare too long to challenge imperious youth will be disposed of in their turn. To display his intellectual as well as physical vitality, Oedipus then also conquers a Sphinx whose "riddle" (the old nursery puzzle about man's successive quadri-, bi-, and tripedal locomotion) he easily solves, and thereby emancipates the Thebans from years of sphincteric terror. For reward he is given the throne of Thebes, vacated by the aging Laius whom Oedipus had slain, and the privilege of marrying the widowed Queen Iocastè.

But nagging doubts remain (who is free of them?), and Oedipus, after more years of restless searching (the curse of Western man), learns from his now aged servant-savior the awful truth that he had indeed killed his father and cohabited incestuously with his mother—"awful" only because he fears that others regard it so. With public histrionics, he blinds (not castrates) himself in expiation (and thereby secures the advantage of being a pathetic rather than a reprehensible figure), and curses his unwanted sons Eteocles and Polynices. He then preempts the lives of his daughters, Antigone and Ismene (as many an aging parent since Agamemnon sacrificed Iphegenia still tries to do) in further wanderings throughout Hellas. Finally, at the Grove of Colonus outside Athens he defies the

Fates and himself becomes a demigod—thus acquiring the archangelic status we all believe is *our* due.

There are, of course, many variations of these legends, not only in Greek, but in Hungarian, Romanian, Finnish, and even Lapland folklore. In one classic version, Homer has Iocastè commit suicide, after which a more sensible Oedipus completes his reign in relative peace. But the stories are never naïvely monothetic; instead, they portray almost every nuance of the imperative, ceaseless seekings that imbue the Western condition—and the temporary triumphs, tantalizing traumata, and terminal tragedies that would be unbearable unless men and women can fancy that they exist in a covertly rational cosmos or else can believe themselves to be superhuman.

## "LATENCY PERIOD"

According to Freud, this lasts from age four or six to puberty, during which interim "instinctual development" is supposedly in abeyance. Actually, however, genital interests continue to evolve, but only as part of experimental play and educational, communicative, peer- and group-orientative exploratory activities through which the child attains its fundamental strengths and skills. These experiences are very important in the formation of character and demand the intelligent, active, participant guidance of parents, teachers, ministers, physicians, and all others entrusted with the care and supervision of children individually or in groups; a laissez faire policy in this regard is often only an excuse for dereliction of duty. On the other hand, it is also true that children cannot be pressed beyond their developed capacities, or channeled into a one-sided exploitation of talent to fulfill familial or tutorial pride.

*Jean Piaget* (1896–), a Swiss philosopher-psychologist, prefers to disregard retrospective or overgeneralized speculations such as the above in favor of careful observations, since verified by others, of the cognitive and manipulative development of children and adolescents, including three of his own. By various ingenious tests, Piaget discerned that an infant assembles various somesthetic *schemata* (for example, "sucking" or "magical seeking") that are later correlated with *external events* that he *introjects, incorporates,* and *assimilates* and to which he eventually *accommodates.* These expanded schemata are in turn progressively combined—although at rates varying with the individual—first into relatively discrete, still egocentric, *preconceptual* sensorimotor responses (birth to 1½ years), then into more integrated, but still monothetic, *pre-operational* thought (to age 11), and finally into complexly *symbolic, multidimensionally, equilibrated,* and relatively logical *formal operations.* The last phase is attained between ages 11 to 15 and developed throughout life to constitute "a one and only space that envelopes the others."

Piaget also describes interdigitating substages for *"magical, linguistic, mathematical* and *moral"* attainments, depending not only on each child's inherent potentialities but also on various important environmental factors that can be manipulated to favor his optimum development. The "mentally retarded" can thus also be rated, not by a misleading and pejorative "IQ," but understood and educated according to their relative status in the Piaget schemata and thus significantly differentiated from infantile autism or childhood schizophrenia.

## Puberty

Although pleasure in genital stimulation is present in both sexes almost from birth, with the maturation of the sex glands (spermatogenesis in boys, ovulation and menarche in girls) sexual drives become more intense. Freud thought that this "reactivated the Oedipus complex" and its concurrent "castration fears" that the still-powerful father would, even at this late date, deprive the child of its sex organs in punishment for the renewed incestuous desires. Whether this is literally the case is dubious, but it is true that although in most Western cultures the boy and girl may be formally initiated into ostensible adulthood through various puberty rites, they are as yet far from adequately prepared for mature responsibilities and still subject to many social limitations and prohibitions, particularly in the sexual sphere. Libidinal urges then find release in various ways:

*Displaced eroticism* in exaggerated dress and hair styles, pornographic literary and pictorial interests, sexually suggestive speech and mannerisms, pelvic-centered dancing to primitive musical rhythms, transient but intense "crushes" on romanticized adolescent or adult figures, etc. Within the customs of time, place, and culture, these are "normal" accompaniments of adolescent exuberance; however, excess in any of them may connote insecurity and escapism from underlying familial, educational, or social anxieties, and may indicate a need for sympathetic counseling, environmental change, and redirection of interests.

*Masturbation,* though physiologically harmless in moderation and almost universally present in both sexes in various forms since infancy, is likely to be of special concern to the sociosexually troubled preadolescent. In this event, misdirected warnings of the supposedly pernicious mental and physical effects of "self-abuse" may arouse persistent and disruptive fears of "loss of manhood," "insanity" or other terrifying consequences, create feelings of excessive shame about supposed external signs of the practice (pallor, acne, etc.), and incite other unfortunate reactions. Masturbation should be explained in realistic terms as an avenue of sexual relief that is generally used less frequently as more completely satisfying heterosexual channelizations are developed, although these should not be encouraged prematurely merely to gratify either parent's jaded or vicarious erotic interests. *Sexual inversions and perversions* may also occur in the form of fetishism, homosexual or heterosexual masturbation, genital-extragenital contacts, or erotic experiences with animals. It must be remembered that such activities are considered deviant only in our Judeo-Christian tradition; in many other cultures, which by all other counts are equally "civilized," variegated sex practices in both young and adult are not only tolerated but expected and do no detectable physical or psychologic harm. However, inasmuch as our children must learn to live in accordance with our own laws and customs, the condemnations and penalties connected with erotic exhibitionisms, seductions, partial or statutory rape, etc., must be made sympathetically but firmly clear, since ignorance in the child will not protect either him or his mentors from adverse social consequences.

# Adolescence

Freud considered basic personal development virtually complete when the "Oedipus complex" was reawakened at puberty and either satisfactorily resolved or again repressed to constitute the unconscious source of characterologic and neurotic deviations. However, the difficult years between puberty and the arbitrary ages of legal "adulthood" constitute an all-important period during which the adolescent must seek and acquire what he will call, often defiantly, his "identity." In our almost incredibly intricate culture, with its multitudes of educational, occupational, esthetic, economic, political, familial, and other intertwined sociotransactional demands and relationships, this acquisition of an adequately multiadaptive yet unique individuality is an increasingly difficult task even for the best-prepared and talented of our youth; consequently, interim or permanent, partial or complete failures are to be expected. These may take the following forms singly or, much more frequently, in various combinations:

## REGRESSIONS

There may be reversions to familial or other dependencies, as expressed in maladjustments at school, financial irresponsibilities, or minor delinquencies requiring repeated interventions and succorances by parents or guardians. These perennial "protectors" and "rescuers" may protest loudly over the injustice of their fate but are often secretly loath to give up their preemptive custody and control of their child whatever his age. Therapy must then include all affected members of the family constellation, if their reciprocally neurotic relationships are to be dealt with and adverse consequences for all concerned prevented. However, strong familial interdependencies, despite current prejudices against them, can also be both practicable and constructive in certain ethnic groups: e.g., the son who from childhood on intends to enter his father's trade or business where he will be best prepared and avidly accepted; the daughter who plans to marry and remain within a happy hegemony. In such instances, only a naïve therapist would try to interfere in the mutual contentment on the grounds that the son or daughter is "immature" or "unemancipated."

STEREOTYPES

If neither normal nor neurotic familial securities seem available or attractive, the late adolescent or young adult may seek status in a peer group that permits a return to ostentatiously neglectful habits of dress and hygiene, "hippie" beards and tangled tresses, idiomatic modes of speech, limited musical and other aesthetic tastes, hideouts in unfurnished shacks or "pads," exhibitionistic sexuality, and pseudosophisticated talk of avant-garde nihilism and social protest. These deviants are in their own jargon more or less "far out"; in contrast, other less escapist groupings are harmless or beneficial as interim experiences throughout youth—and indeed continue into normal adulthood in the form of cliques and societies with their prescribed uniforms, secret handclasps, passwords, rituals, and public professions of high social purpose sometimes leading to actual public service. The dividing line is this: When an adolescent becomes so immersed in "extracurricular activities" as to neglect his education, physical health, and broader social development, or when he selects a group advocating "sports" that endanger others (dueling, drag racing), promoting public obscenity, sexual arrogance, and physical violence, indulging in escapes from reality through alcohol, "goof balls" (dexedrine), "red bullets" (seconal), "pot" (marijuana), even more deleterious "psychedelic" drugs such as mescaline, lysergic acid, methedrine ("speed"), or the opiates morphine or heroin, then comprehensive therapy directed toward resolving physical, familial, and group insecurities, revealing newer opportunities, and inculcating more practicable social loyalties and modes of conduct is urgently called for. This may, when necessary, be coordinated with familial, institutional, or even police discipline until healthy internal restraints and external adaptations are developed.

Are "psychedelic" drugs harmful? The answer to this incidental but highly pertinent question obviously depends on whether any drug can really be considered sufficiently "mind-expanding" or "inspirational" to overcompensate for its dangers. Many drugs have had their advocates on this score. Long before De Quincey wrote his *Confessions*, Lao-Tze praised the narcotizing "poppy of philosophy," Galen prescribed Samian clay to meliorate melancholy and clear consciousness, and our Navajo and Potawatami Indians had traditionally greeted the Great Spirit with peyote and mescal. Stephen Foster claimed he could not compose his songs nor Edgar Allan Poe his poetry without the activating alchemy of alcohol. Freud was long convinced of the inspirational properties of cocaine, and Churchill insisted that he wrote and spoke best under the optimum synergism of nicotine and whiskey. For that matter, we know full well that smoking and drinking are harmful; nevertheless, most of us still believe that a cocktail and cigar make us feel more alert, imaginative, and creative. The use of nepenthics, then, like our sexual mores, is a relative rather than an absolute problem, and it is mainly by sheer numbers that adult consumers of alcohol and tranquilizers outvote and condemn the votaries of marijuana and other drugs that, speaking from the standpoint of overall comprehensive social welfare, are considerably less disruptive.

However, not altogether so. According to L. M. Zunin (1969), the harmful effects of marijuana can include (1) unpredictability of response, (2) distortion of time and space perception, (3) sleepiness and apathy, (4) decreased awareness of oneself, (5) mild motor uncoordination, (6) impaired intellectual functioning, (7) emotional lability, (8) disinhibition and decreased control over judgment and critical censorship, (9) psychologic dependence, (10) transient and occasionally permanent emotional disorders, (11) variable appetite, (12) gastrointestinal and respiratory ailments, (13) a predilection for more potent stimulants and narcotics, and (14) the necessity to deal with illegal channels of supply and criminal elements of our society.

But even granted that, because of its low content of tetra-hydrocannabinol, "pot" or "grass" is not as harmul as the above catechism might indicate, are not LSD, methaqualone, methe-drine, and other "psychedelics" to which many marijuana smokers "progress" far more dangerous? Present evidence indicates that these drugs are indeed exceedingly treacherous. Laurea found that 13 percent of chronic drug users experience overwhelming panic, 12 percent become violent, 9 percent suicidal, and 10 percent require extended hospitalization. Ungerleider *et al.* reported that "bad trips" in the Los Angeles area immediately, or as recurrences long after ingestion of LSD, now exceed hospital facilities even for emergency care; that there is no reliable antidote for LSD toxicosis; and that unpredictable suicides, homicides, and psychoses requiring months of hospitalization are becoming tragically frequent even after a single dose of the drug. Nor may the effects end with the user: Irwin and Egoscue have detected *in vivo* chromosomal abnormalities in LSD habitués that can endanger the welfare of future generations. Although this last effect has been questioned by Laughman, Warkany, Takacs, *et al.*, the total increasing use of alcohol, sedatives, stimulants, and narcotics by our young has be-come an urgent and sometimes tragic problem.

And yet this must be taken in the sober context of a general social tendency. Of the 70 million adult Americans who use alcohol, no less than eight million drink it to harmful excess; in addition, we take thirteen billion doses of amphetamines and barbiturates annually. Nor can we forget the untold tons of so-called tran-quilizers, ataractics, and antidepressants we avidly consume with or without benefit of prescription, especially since, as Esrig and others warn, they can induce convulsions, delirium, and death either directly or during withdrawal. Conversely, Freedman and Jaffe estimate that the great majority of those who try LSD never take a second dose, whereas, according to Cohen, the minimum lethal dose of the drug is so great that in one case 15,000 micrograms given with homicidal intent were not fatal. Nevertheless, despite the rationalization of those avid for them, no drug has been shown to be of any objective aid in creativity, and carefully controlled studies have proved that none of the "psychedelics" is really useful in any form of physical or psychiatric therapy except possibly for the dying patient. Since, on the other hand, marijuana, LSD, the amphetamines and related substances do have unpredictable and sometimes devastating side effects and may lead to tragic experiments with "harder" drugs [federal agents estimate that there are one hundred thousand teen-age "horse" (heroin) addicts in New York City alone, of which five hundred die annually from overdoses], the moral justification for using any of these drugs "to expand the horizons of the human mind" is wishfully illusory and medically dangerous.

SEXUAL PROMISCUITY

The connotations of "promiscuity" vary widely even among Western cultures: In the Scandinavian lands, for example, teen-agers in the upper social strata are expected to have lovers and mistresses; over 40 percent of pregnancies are conceived outside of marriage, and all children born out of wedlock are raised by the state without onus of illegitimacy. In our own country, sexual customs are changing rapidly under pressure from our iconoclastic youth: Formal "dating," often encouraged by upper-middle-class parents, now frequently begins at puberty; "going steady" with a succession of two- or three-month partners is a status symbol in many a juvenile group and often involves "necking" or "petting" (including fondling of breasts and genitals) or "making out" to the extent of sexual intercourse. If and when these practices become even more widely and frankly accepted, the adolescent's fears of social reprisal will correspondingly diminish, but because of the inherent uncertainties and insecurities of this age period in our culture, the poignant rivalries, jealousies, disappointments, and reactive hostilities involved will often require sympathetic hearings, interim reassurances, and active guidance toward more practicable, mature, and gratifying relationships.

IDENTITY DIFFUSION

This term refers to another unfortunate eventuality during high school and early college years: With so many competing demands and conflictful roles to play, the late adolescent may spread himself thin trying to be simultaneously a compliant child, a brilliant scholar, a winning athlete, a popular leader, a cryptic mystic, a potent lover or seductive nymph, a cynical yet "socially involved" sophisticate, and a dozen other incompatible alteregos. The result is often a fragile superficiality in each role, and at worst, chaos and breakdown in all. As noted, this may be prevented in the pre-adolescent period by optimal collaboration between parents and teachers in guiding the child in accordance with his individual limitations, motivations, and potentialities. Such combined counsels must be continued at higher levels of academic and occupational planning and more specific preparations for attainable and compatible professional, social, and familial careers in adulthood.

CASE 13 Borderline Delinquency

Fairly direct and consistent measures of reorientation and mentorship are occasionally necessary, as recommended in the following letter to a troubled colleague who requested a consultation.

Dear Dr. ———:
　　Your seventeen-year-old nephew K.N. can be characterized briefly: about as badly spoiled, self-willed, and undisciplined a perennial pubescent as I've had in the office lately. Unfortunately, he has learned all the standard techniques of seducing and controlling his parents—particularly his wishfully gullible mother—and is firmly convinced that these will serve him indefinitely everywhere. Some of his misinterpretations of reality border on the schizoid, but his main patterns of escapism, indulgence, bravado, and explosive

aggression when frustrated are sociopathic and still possibly reversible.

His treatment, of course, will have to be directed as much to his family as himself, along the following lines:

1.  Simple explanations, avoiding all technical terms and medical implications, of his need to learn different character patterns and external adjustments.
2.  Insistence on regular hours, a job, social decency, etc. to be encouraged by set predictable rewards or enforced by inevitable punishments.
3.  Failing adequate control at home, an adequate boarding school with psychiatric help or trial of military service.
4.  Failing that, legal commitment for therapy before, rather than after, he develops more serious delinquencies.

I made this as plain as I could to all concerned within the limitations of time and tact, and referred them back to you. But, without the cooperation of all concerned, I doubt that I can be of further help.

CASE 14 Another consultation in a case of Adolescent Delinquency Protracted into Adulthood

Dear Dr. ———:

Mr. T. presents a case history instructive enough for a monograph: a preemptively demanding and covertly hostile dependent who perverted the "classical analytic technique" of one of our own colleagues to his own neurotic advantage for many years, leading to the inevitably bitter and possibly tragic payoff. I am not sure he can be rehabilitated at this late day; but if therapy is at all possible, it would now have to take the following lines:

Interviews with his wife, brother, and associates to lessen their victimization and diminish the important—and quite conscious—dependency and aggressive gains he is now deriving from his "illness" and its consequent need for interminable "analysis."

A radical change in technique away from "dream analysis," "symbolic interpretations," and escapist regression to a quite literal and practical concern with present activities and tenable future goals. Should he temporarily revert to a dramatic and invaliding "psychosis," a small sanitarium with no electroshock therapy, but with few privileges or visitors either, would be indicated.

These and other considerations speak against his coming from Milwaukee to Chicago for therapy, since he would use the three days a week "off" as another officially sponsored escape into irresponsibility, fogged by "free-associative" double-talk. I have therefore recommended that he return to you and that I discuss his progress with you and see him only occasionally as you direct. I have had fairly extensive and successful experience with many such cases that have come to me after years of such misguided "analysis," and perhaps I can, on your occasional visits to Chicago, help you a bit with this one.

All these predisposing circumstances are outweighed by a far more overwhelming apprehension: namely, that many of our perceptive youth currently believe that *they have no future worth having unless our outmoded social order is promptly and radically changed* by peaceful or, if necessary, by drastic means. With our country in the early 1970s still dominated by a firmly institutionalized military-industrial-trade-union complex that demands eighty billion dollars a year of our national budget and consumes over 12 percent of our total national product; with a standing army of three and a half million men and women who, in the name of patriotism, are being trained to commit acts of civilian as well as military destruction for which we ourselves condemned and executed Nazi criminals at Nuremberg; with the most intensive and least discriminating program of "peacetime" conscription in the history of any democratic country even yet constituting a hazard to every young man's future; with odds for a global nuclear holocaust still estimated to be about 1 in 3 by 1990 and about even by 2000— thousands of our youth, whatever their "race," "class," or other convictions, consider their currently prescribed educational and other disciplines as leading to a chaotic rather than a creative life, and labor under a sense of not-so-quiet desperation that sometimes finds deviant or violent expressions.

## Sexual and Marital Problems

Many marriages are being contracted at or near the minimal age limits by couples who, under the guise of undertaking mutual marital responsibilities, are really seeking dependent securities, social approbation of sexual license, and variously rationalized escapes from the necessity of more thorough preparations for mature accomplishments. Under these circumstances, disappointments and dissatisfactions are inevitable and give rise to intense anxieties, depressions, or periods of diffuse restlessness with accompanying insomnia, cardiac palpitations, gastrointestinal disorders and other disturbances of bodily function, attempts at relief through drugs and alcohol, and sexual frigidity or impotence usually limited to the spouse. With regard to the latter difficulty, it is a peculiar aspect of our present culture that in many circles a preoccupation with sexuality has become so fashionable that partners in a poorly planned and conducted marriage, after a few days to as many decades of recurrent crises, will come to the therapist with the naïve plea that if only their "sexual problems" can be solved—including their needs for escapist or covertly punitive extramarital homosexual or heterosexual adventures—their marriage "could still somehow be worked out." Accordingly, a specific request is often made for instruction in "sexual techniques," in the illusion that this would form a solid basis for marital compatibility.

CASE 15 Legal Consultation in Divorce Proceedings

> To: Mr. Z. and Mr. A., Attorneys
> Subject: Mr. and Mrs. E.
>
> As is ethical in such consultations, it is understood (a) that the following report of my examinations will omit all data that either Mr. or Mrs. E. wished to be kept confidential, (b) that the conclusions reached will have relevance only to the problem of their marital compatibility, and (c) that no portion of this report be made available to any person other than the parties concerned and their counselors.

MR. S.F.E., AGE 34

> Mr. E. arrived nearly forty minutes late for his appoint-

ment, remarked casually that tardiness was one of his lifelong customs, and was thereafter quite vague, evasive, or stereotyped in his communications. Nevertheless, enough data were gathered for a psychiatric summary.

*Personal History.* Mr. E's father died when Mr. E. was only 10 years old, leaving nine children ranging in age from 19 to one year old to the care of Mr. E's mother. Under these adverse familial and economic conditions, Mr. E. developed a somewhat overcompensatory ambitiousness coupled with a lack of self-discipline and social coordination— a combination that resulted in marginal adjustments at school, in a long series of failures at various jobs, and recent difficulties in his religious affiliations. Corresponding tendencies to grandiosity, irresponsibility, and escapism also affected his marital adjustments; for example, he quit his job just before his wedding in 1947 and lived 10 years in a two-and-a-half-room flat on his wife's income, because he refused to work steadily for a series of employers or in his own business ventures. He was away playing golf when his wife delivered their only daughter, now age 10. He insisted on more children despite his wife's fears of repeated miscarriages and their continuous poverty and indebtedness; and he was home as little as possible because, only two years after their marriage, he "could no longer stand her nagging and her tempers and her always diminishing me—and her damned interfering sister." When at his wife's insistence, they finally bought a home some 18 months ago he threatened that he "would burn it down around her ears if she didn't have more children." However, when their conflicts increased instead of abated in the new environment, he left her and the child a year ago and now wants a divorce.

*Mental Status.* Mr. E. has normal intelligence without signs of organic impairment, but he is emotionally unstable and deeply insecure in many ways. For example, he wavers between confessions of abject failure and overreactive self-importance, between passive dependency and blustering aggressivity, semifanatic religiosity and cynical agnosticism, and pathetic indecision and stubborn intransigence. The latter attitude currently is crystallized into a sullen rejection of his wife but extends also into interpersonal remoteness and increasingly antisocial postures. These processes now constitute a serious character neurosis that may progressively handicap all of Mr. E.'s life adjustments; however, he has little insight into his own pecularities and almost no current desire to seek help for them.

MRS. E.K.E., AGE 36

*Personal History.* Mrs. E's father died when she was five years old, and her mother a decade later, leaving her to be protected, perhaps excessively, by a sister nine years older than herself. Mrs. E.'s early scholastic, social, sexual, and occupational adaptations, though not as marginal as those of her husband, also showed areas of maladjustment; she entered marriage with almost as little clear forethought and realistic planning as did her husband. When the inevitable conflicts over money, family, sex, children, etc. occurred in rapid succession and increasing intensity, her reactions took the form of complaints, tempers, and hysterics, setting up cycles of sulking, absences, and periods of separation during the past six years. Since the last one three years ago, she has returned to work and has acquired insistent suitors. However, she finds her "marriage failure" unpleasant and wants to "try him out again because my daughter still loves him, and we know he is emotionally sick."

*Mental Status.* Superficially, Mrs. E. is more warm, friendly, communicative, and receptive than her husband, though she soon reveals a quite similar tendency to headstrong self-righteousness and blames nearly all of her difficulties on others. This stand includes the saving grace of (a) considering Mr. E. "sick" and (b) offering to undertake therapy for her own lesser "nervousness" if he would do the same in a joint effort to save their marriage. Unfortunately, this offer is also part of a covert bid for implicit victory in their many conflicts, though it may be more constructively employed by a skillful therapist.

*Recommendations.* Present indications are that unless Mr. and Mrs. E. undertake effective treatment for their respective personality difficulties, any rapprochement between them would be short-lived and would only add to their current conflicts and the emotional traumata imposed on their daughter. Mrs. E. professes to agree to such therapy but, if—as is likely—Mr. E. refuses, renewed frictions, separations, and an ultimate divorce seem inevitable. In that case Mrs. E. seems capable of caring for her daughter, whereas Mr. E.'s visitation rights should depend on the reliability and rationality of his future conduct.

CASE  16  Marital Discord in Later Years—Psychiatric Consultation Requested by the Court of Domestic Relations

MRS. M.C., AGE 56

Mrs. C. admits that her emotional insecurities and hypersensitivities date to her childhood, when she was raised by an invalid mother who suffered from "hysterical fevers" during the father's prolonged absences from home. Nevertheless, she completed a fair education, worked steadily, maintained her marriage faithfully for 32 years, "raised and married off" her only daughter (who has now four children of her own), and even helped support her husband during his long periods of his illness by piecework at home until a year ago. At that time, however, she discovered he was having occasional sexual relations with a neighbor's middle-aged wife and, in reaction, developed a chronic depressive state characterized by fatigue, loss of weight (down to 100 lbs.), frequent crying spells, and a maintained mood of suspicion and recrimination. Four months ago, after many broken promises and ensuing quarrels, she sued for divorce "to see if the shock would change him"; since it did not, she now confides that without letting Mr. C. know, she has confronted her husband's paramour and plans to "sue her for alienation of affections just to see what he will do then."

*Mental Status.* Mrs. C. is a cooperative and fairly intelligent woman who, unfortunately, seems to have been exceedingly disturbed by what she considers a recent and devastating assault on her fragile security system. In overreaction, she has harassed her husband excessively with suspicions and demands and by her own retreat into a variably agitated and hostile, melancholic state. Her present plans to "test" her husband by new hreats and suits are correspondingly unrealistic and confused, being compounded of motives of revenge and a contrary fear of being totally deserted and helpless at her present age unless she can frighten him into compliance. She has partly recognized this irrationality and has occasionally sought help from physicians. She has also made single visits to two psychiatrists but obviously needs more thorough and consistent guidance.

### MR. I.C., AGE 62

Mr. C.'s personal history is here irrelevant other than that he apparently never developed truly deep and consistent feelings of responsibility and loyalty toward anyone, including his wife. His affair with a neighbor began casually as a reassertio⌐ of aging virility some 18 months ago; it was admittedly not occasioned by any actions or deficiencies on the part of his wife other than that she was not invariably sexually responsive. Since then, however, he feels very bitter about her "nagging and crying and calling me up all the time; if she'd just leave me alone things would probably work out by themselves." He intends neither to marry nor to leave his paramour but at the same time wishes to retain his marriage— with just a "period of separation so I can have some time to myself." Naturally, he desires his wife to drop all accusations and suits immediately and feels martyred that she does not do so.

*Mental Status.* Mr. C., too, has intellectual capacities within normal range, but his exercise of them, especially in the current situation, is handicapped by long-term personality characteristics of recalcitrance, thoughtless and sometimes arrogant self-seeking, insensitivity to the feelings of others, a tendency toward conscious hypocrisy, and resort to frank hostility when not given his own way in interpersonal dealings. He, too, regards a divorce as eventually inconvenient yet, despite half-hearted disclaimers, feels no contrition about his past behavior or any sincere desire to alter it except under direct threat of punishment.

*Recommendations.* In view of the currently incompatible motivations and interactions of Mr. and Mrs. C. it is probable that a period of directed separation would do little toward really healing the breach; after the usual mutual promises the same or similar conflicts would soon recur between them. Divorce and ensuing litigations would be no less futile in giving either of them stable satisfactions. One course would be to refer each for competent marital counseling, with or without temporary separation; if they agree and the Court assents, I shall be happy to help them arrange it. In any case they will probably rejoin each other eventually, since neither has much of an alternative.

## Case 17 A Contest for Middle-Age Control

Herewith the reports on Mr. and Mrs. L.S., both age 55. From a psychological standpoint, neither really wants a divorce, since each basically needs the other. Unfortunately, however, with each the conflict has now become a matter of personal prestige and dominance: Mrs. S., consciously or not, has the attitude that if she acceded to her husband's sexual and other demands before he gave up drinking she would lose status and control; Mr. S. feels that drinking and sex are indispensable trappings to mask his fears of inferiority. The solution would be to make each feel personal satisfaction rather than supposed defeat in a reconciliation—a task in which your Court has long experience. As to Mr. S.'s drinking, I can help him control that, if he so desires, with Antabuse and other appropriate therapy.

## The Role of Sex in Therapy

A request for instruction in social technique need not place the therapist in a dilemma. He is aware that sexual diversions have always been sought by men and women as a temporary relief from life's stresses and have throughout history been expressed in pseudotherapeutic cults. One need only recall the paleolithic Venuses, the temple rites of Ishtar in ancient Mesopotamia, the orgiastic Dionysian Mysteries of Greek and Roman times, and the open lasciviousness of later generations as celebrated by Petronius, Boccaccio, Rabelais, or Mailer.[1] Today, also, defensively "romanticized" or cynically "sophisticated" erotic defiances and escapisms

[1] An intriguing example of what might be called erototherapy in the last century was the Celestial Bed in Dr. James Graham's Temple of Health in London, an "Institution Dedicated to the Cure of All Diseases," and thus advertised to bachelors and benedicts of both sexes in the Madison Avenue panegyrics of seven score years ago:

"The Grand Celestial Bed, whose medical influences are now celebrated from Pole to Pole and from the Rising to the Setting of the Sun, is twelve feet long by nine feet wide, supported by Forty Pillars of brilliant glass of

are sought in frenetic mate-combinations and permutations, not only by our restless youth, but also by the harassed minor executives and den mothers of split-level suburbia. Nevertheless, when a disillusioned supplicant insists that his or her difficulties, however avidly or salaciously described, are "basically sexual," experienced therapists have learned to put aside the perhaps somewhat voyeuristic interests that they may have formerly rationalized as searchingly scientific and to explore, instead, the more significant issues of the underlying insecurities, dependencies, frustrated ambitions, fears, hostilities, ambiguous values and social goals, or other spheres of conflict and uncertainty inadequately covered by the seven veils of sexuality. When these more fundamental problems are solved through various forms of dynamic, comprehensive, reality-oriented dyadic or group therapy (which, not infrequently, may have to include self-seeking marital or extramarital partners, interfering friends and families, and even contentious attorneys), the sexual difficulties, which are usually secondary defensive, escapist, or compensatory epiphenomena, disappear with predictable and gratifying regularity.

## Adult Psychosomatic Disorders

As has been experimentally as well as clinically demonstrated, conflicts of adaptation are reflected not only in aberrations of individual and social conduct but also in physiologic dysfunctions that vary with the constitution of the individual and the nature of

---

the most exquisite workmanship in richly variegated colors. . . . On the uppermost summit of the dome are placed two exquisite figures of Cupid (Eros) and Psyche, with a figure of Hymen behind . . . supporting a Celestial Crown sparkling over a pair of great loving turtle-doves on a little bed of roses. . . . At the head of the bed appears, sparkling with electrical fire, the Great First (*sic!*) Commandment: 'Be fruitful, multiply and replenish the earth!' "

The notice went on to imply that suitable personnel would be furnished as required—thus anticipating the use of expert "wife surrogates" in the therapy of impotence in single males as recently advocated in the book *Human Sexual Inadequacy* by Masters and Johnson.

the stress. These disorders may include high blood pressure (*hypertension*) with its concomitant arteriosclerosis and impaired vital circulation to the brain, heart, and kidneys; gastric hyperacidity and pyloric spasms that may lead to peptic ulcer formation; muscular strains that may render the joints arthritic; and other disturbances of function that can result in serious organic disease. As also noted, the person under stress may have sought surcease in excessive amounts of alcohol, sedatives, tranquilizers and opiates and could be suffering from the adverse effects of these drugs up to and including the excited, hallucinated, delusional, exhaustive, and potentially lethal states of acute delirium or chronic toxic psychosis. Under these circumstances, therapy either must be directed exclusively by a physician competent to treat the physiologic, pharmacologic, and pathologic complications by medical or, if necessary, emergency surgical means, or must be conducted in close collaboration with a medical consultant.

CASE 18 Brief Therapy in a Gross Stress Reaction with Alcoholic Delirium—The Problem of Masochism

> The patient, a twenty-seven-year-old man, was admitted to the university hospital in acute alcoholic delirium—disoriented, ridden by fearful hallucinations, and confusedly amnestic. He made a rapid recovery in two days of rest, mild sedation, hydrotherapy, and high caloric feeding and was then able to give a consistent account of his life experiences. Briefly, the history revealed that at an early age he had suffered from severe rheumatic fever that left him with painful joints and impaired cardiac function. The father—a self-reliant and highly religious but apparently ignorant and unfeeling man— had then taken a strong dislike to his "weakling" son and had placed numerous obstacles in the way of the latter's schooling, including almost impossibly high requirements as to scholastic performance to compensate for his athletic deficiencies.[1]

---

[1] Although it is only indirectly relevant to the main theme of this case, it may be noted that the patient, like many others with deep resentments of a tyrannical parent repressed beneath a thick layer of fearful compliance, equated intellectual performance with virility and was anxiously ambivalent

Despite all handicaps, including the necessity for partial self-support, the patient completed junior college and, later, special training for an accountant's certificate. The strain, however, told on his health, and at the age of 21 he again fell seriously ill, was diagnosed as having moderately advanced apical tuberculosis, and was sent to a municipal sanatorium. He took even this serious setback with good grace, cooperated well in his treatment, and was making a fair recovery when he became enamored of a girl who had herself recovered from mild tuberculosis and was about to leave the sanatorium. Understandably fearful of losing her, the patient persuaded the hospital physician—who apparently in this instance let his romantic paternalism affect his medical judgment—to permit their joint discharge, and the couple were married soon after.

Misfortunes, however, promptly began to pile up, at a rate that would not be given credence outside the Book of Job. The patient's wife, dissatisfied with his salary as a bank clerk, insisted that he resume his study for a CPA examination, and the patient, in his devotion to her, again taxed his strength and resistance dangerously. A defalcation was next discovered in the bank's accounts, and for several harrowing weeks the patient was under unjust suspicion. During this period, while he was suspended from his job and under technical bail, his wife left him with no explanation other than a note to the effect that she "couldn't any longer tolerate a physical weakling and especially a thief." Two days after this, the patient was completely cleared of all responsibility in the bank theft, only to be told by the bank manager who had originally accused him that, "for obvious reasons," the two could no longer work together and that the patient would therefore have to resign his position. That night, in a fit of coughing, the patient for the first time in months brought up blood-streaked sputum—a strong indication that his tuberculosis was reactivated, and quite probably more seriously than ever. With everything gone—job, wife and even marginal

---

about both. Thus autoerotism was accompanied by dreads that it would weaken his intelligence, and he struggled to avoid masturbating during term examinations so that, by reporting good grades to his father, he would not incur the latter's wrath.

health—the patient gravely considered suicide, but then came to a preliminary decision: Since sober habits, hard study, honest work and faithful devotion had brought nothing but frustration and sorrow, before he died he was going to have an orgy, however brief, of defiant self-indulgence. Not knowing quite how to go about this, he collected all his available funds and began with what he had heard the men at his office boast of—he went to a locally notorious saloon, picked out one of the more expensive "hostesses," and, for the first time in his life, set out to get drunk. His companion proved very receptive to the idea, and after the first few drinks she bought a plentiful supply of liquor with his money, and accompanied him home. There she continued to ply him with drink for another day until he was in a confused stupor—after which she appropriated a considerable fee for her services and left him to his own devices. The next day the patient was found in a state of agitated delirium by a neighbor who had previously liked the patient as an unobtrusive, friendly person, and who now rightly reasoned that he "must be out of his mind to act this way." Fortunately, the neighbor refrained from calling the police ambulance and instead brought the patient to the university hospital for medical care.

TREATMENT

The patient's therapy was first designed to meet his urgent medical needs and then directed toward his immediate social rehabilitation. A tuberculosis specialist, called into consultation, diagnosed some reactivation of his pulmonary tuberculosis but, fortunately, was able to control it quite successfully by a partial pneumothorax. The cardiac lesion was similarly checked and found to be sufficiently compensated to permit the patient a considerable latitude of activity. The psychiatrist then took an active role in helping the patient reorganize his affairs. The bank manager was summoned for an interview and came, as was to be expected, partly out of curiosity and partly in a defensively patronizing "I-knew-he-was-queer-all-the-time" attitude. Nevertheless, the psychiatrist, while ostensibly appealing to the manager's humanitarian sympathies, tacitly implied that if the patient remained embittered, he might also take legal action; this thought evoked sufficient concern to induce the manager, with a slightly harried air of "Let's let bygones be bygones" to re-employ the patient at an increased salary. Next, the patient's wife was similarly interviewed, and her own needs for security and fear of friendless ill health utilized in a manner not only to effect a reconciliation with her husband but also to make more probable somewhat greater interdependence and consequent harmony in their financial, sexual, and social interrelationships. With his most pressing problems thus partially resolved, the patient was discharged from the hospital, but with preset arrangements for interviews at weekly intervals to help guide him through the inevitable difficulties of his readjustments and to guard against renewed tendencies to overreactive ambition and overintensive effort. When seen in a follow-up interview a year later, he reported that he had passed his accountancy examinations, had been promoted to the position of teller at the bank, was fairly happy in his work and in his marriage, and had experienced no further serious difficulties.

## Psychosomatic Diagnoses

The question is often raised, "How does one determine whether an illness is emotional or organic?" The query assumes that the cause of every illness must be *either* "emotional" or "organic"—a misleading oversimplification when it implies that "ruling out" one alternative proves the existence of the other. The diagnostic problem is not the differentiation of "psychologic" from "physical" factors but a careful survey of the *interplay* of all of the external adaptational and internal physiologic influences that together determine the patient's symptoms. For that matter, in the everincomplete state of our medical knowledge and skills, "negative physical and laboratory findings" do *not* "rule out organic illness," let alone prove that the patient's complaints are "purely functional" or "completely neurotic"—depending upon which pejorative phrase is preferred. On the contrary, if a clinical disorder is to be attributed even in part to "psychogenic" causes, *positive diagnostic criteria,* almost as specific as those for the organic components of disease, must be present. Briefly, the criteria are these:

PRESENCE OF ANXIETY

In the psychiatric sense, this represents a recurrent or continuous excess of apprehension, which sometimes reaches the intensity of panic. As described in the earlier section on diagnosis, there may be an almost unmistakable *anxiety syndrome:* cardiac palpitations, rapid irregular respirations, constrictive sensations in the thorax ("a load on the chest") or in the throat (*globus hystericus*), variable flushings and sweatings, "butterflies in the stomach" (*splanchnic constrictions*), muscular tensions and tremors, or—much more rarely these days, even in women—fainting (*hysterical syncope*), with loss of sphincter control.

CASE 19 Political Subversion—Counteraggressive Anxiety

A twenty-two-year-old laborer complained of typical and severe anxiety attacks that had begun two months previously and that he attributed to "heart disease from overwork." The history revealed that he had been raised in privation in the slums of a steel town, had received relatively little formal education, and had grown up with strong resentments against an economic system that, he felt, sentenced him to a life of squalor and drudgery. These resentments had been intensified by his first few years of work in the steel mills until the patient, seeking group support for his social hostilities, joined a fascist political cell pledged to a program of violent revolution. In accordance with the party plan, he was assigned to remain and, if possible, advance himself in the steel mill so that he "could work and then strike from the inside." When the war came, however, circumstances changed rapidly in a way that made the patient's attitudes toward his job and his employers considerably more ambivalent. Because of his native skill and intelligence, he was given relatively profitable work amid favorable surroundings. When he proved his competence, he was classified as "essential laborer" and so saved from being inducted into serving a country toward which he felt little allegiance. Finally, he was given the best-paying and most responsible job available at his level of employment—operating a huge crane that transferred iron ore from a lake freighter to an open-hearth furnace. The patient gloried in this work as long as his instructor was with him to prevent any mistakes in operation. However, the first day he was trusted alone in the control turret he began to experience severe anxiety that soon centered on a single obsessional thought: With one pull of a lever he could so manipulate his gargantuan machine as to sink the ship, wreck the furnace, and probably kill several dozen men. As he pictured this his heart pounded, his hands trembled, his vision blurred, and his knees grew weak; finally, these subjective and physiologic manifestations of his fears grew so severe that he applied for sick leave and entered the clinics.

### THERAPY

This consisted of a thorough physical examination (conducted mainly so that complete reports as to the patient's physical health could be sent to his employers), protective rest, and sedation. With sympathetic understanding and guidance, the patient—an intelligent and essentially honest individual—was then led to recognize that his anxieties and obsessions had their origins in conflicts among his lifelong aggressions, counterpoised inhibitions, and recently altered group loyalties. As insight deepened and new securities in therapeutic and social relationships were found, his obsessive fears diminished rapidly. Fortunately, too, his hostilities were further disarmed when the company he had worked for proved entirely cooperative in paying his hospital fees, giving him an interim vacation, and then offering him a choice of several jobs. The patient returned to work, found his duties as a ground-gang foreman almost entirely to his liking, and has remained symptom-free.

### REACTIONS TO ANXIETY

Anxiety, then, characteristically occurs when, explicitly or not, the patient apprehends some actual or symbolic danger to his identity, integrity, or control: in other instances, an impending examination at school, a disappointment in love, or a promotion to responsibilities he wishes to avoid. Conversely, anxiety is mitigated when the overt or covert stress is diminished, as when an unwanted engagement is broken, a more congenial occupation is secured, or a heterosexual threat is dissipated.

PSYCHASTHENIC PATTERNS

Since severe anxiety is intolerable, the patient is likely to develop various adaptive maneuvers that are fairly easily recounted on direct inquiry. The most common are:

*phobias:* persistent fears that may appear excessive or unreasonable to the lay observer, but that help the patient to avoid heights, crowds, sexual temptations, or other situations or relationships he regards as symbolically threatening;

*obsessions:* recurrent preoccupations with erotic, dependent, aggressive, or other persistent thoughts and fantasies; and

*compulsions:* seemingly aimless but insistently repetitive acts such as touching, counting, or other rituals. The patient invariably protests that he cannot control these reactions, in that any attempt to act counter to his phobias, obsessions, or compulsions immediately occasions renewed anxiety.

CASE 20 Counteraggressive Compulsion

A successful executive who, for various reasons, unconsciously hated the responsibilities of marriage and fatherhood was troubled many times a day with the idea that his two children by his divorced wife were somehow ill or in danger, although he knew them to be safe in a well-run private school to which he himself took them every morning. As a result, he felt impelled to interrupt his office routine thrice daily to make personal calls to the school authorities. After several months the principal began to question the sincerity of the patient's fatherly solicitude and thus intensified his obsessive–compulsive rituals by bringing the issue more nearly into the open. The same patient could not return home at night unless he brought a small present to his second wife and each of his children, although, significantly, it was almost always something they did not want.

CASE 21 Phobic–Compulsive Behavior

The son of a forceful business executive was so afraid of tall buildings, which to him were unconsciously symbolic of his father's threatening power and authority, that he could not

visit the center of the city—including the physician's office—
unless led by the hand by a protective father-surrogate such
as a close relative or a male nurse.

## NEUROMUSCULAR AND SOMATIC DISTURBANCES

Sensorimotor (*hysterical*) or internal organic (*psychosomatic*)
dysfunctions can be recognized as predominantly psychogenic by
the following characteristics: They do not resemble those produced
by any probable combination of organic lesions. Examples are loss
of sensation solely in the hands and feet (*glove-and-shoe anesthesia*),
a professed inability to sit or walk without loss of strength in any
extremity (*astasia-abasia*), triple vision, etc.

The complaints tend to shift from one organ system to another,
and vary with the intensity of intercurrent emotional rather than
physical stresses.

The specific dysfunctions are often symbolically or semanti-
cally determined. This may be relatively obvious: for instance,
an "hysterical paralysis" of the arms in a woman who has severely
beaten her child, or a peptic ulcer in a professedly self-reliant
patient whose stomach reflects his repressed hunger for maternal
care and feeding by its excessive secretions and prehensile spasms.
On the other hand the significance may be obscure, as in the
debilitating invalidism of *anorexia nervosa,* which may keep an
extremely dependent patient physically, sexually, and socially infantile and thereby compel attention and sustenance.

Conversely, as in the case of anxiety reactions "spontaneous"
symptomatic ameliorations may occur when the stresses are
removed, as on vacations, after a fortunate turn in the patient's
familial, economic, or social status, or after more covert
gratifications.

### SECONDARY GAINS

In addition to these primary determinants, the patient may
also be deriving ancillary (epinosic) advantages from his neurotic
illness: i.e., monetary rewards or avoidance of scholastic, military,
or other duties. However, these seemingly self-evident explanations,

despite the cynicism with which they are often advanced, rarely in themselves account adequately for the patient's covertly cherished disabilities and escapisms, which he may sacrifice his career and fortune to maintain.

As noted, a sympathetic attitude and a few tactful questions by the therapist will nearly always elicit a wealth of information about the patient's past and current behavior that will strengthen the probability that his present illness, too, is largely neurotic. Thus, if he came from an unstable home, or developed early and persistent difficulties in his educational, social, sexual, and occupational adjustments, or had vague and frequent complaints for which he consulted not only many physicians but a spate of chiropractors, naturopaths, and faith healers, all of whom helped him only temporarily, and if his present symptoms are once again occasioned by typical personal and social maladjustments—then his current illness is all the more likely to be another episode in a long series of evasive, hypochondriac, regressive, and invaliding reactions that he has made an integral part of his neurotic way of life.

Therapeutically, immediate though usually temporary improvement may be induced by suggestion, placebos, or hypnosis— although (see p. 172), the last is often unwise or, in medical terms *contraindicated*. In the longer run, however, if the patient responds favorably to friendly rapport, relinquishes his doubts, fears, and conflicts, accepts reasonable explanations and gentle guidance, develops better orientations and values (*insight*), and uses these to achieve more favorable intrapersonal and social adjustments— and if at the same time his symptoms show a corresponding improvement—then his illness can *post hoc* logically be considered to have been due in part to "emotional" causes.

CASE 22 Sensorimotor    Neurosis—Brief    Psychotherapy    by Sigmund Freud

> Bruno Walter, in his autobiography, relates that early in his career he developed such pain and limitations of motion in his shoulder that his future as a symphony conductor seemed threatened. A series of physicians could find little physically

wrong with him, and since other treatments were ineffective, he was finally advised to consult Sigmund Freud in Vienna.

This Walter did with considerable trepidation since, although he himself suspected that his difficulty was non-organic, he nevertheless dreaded the prospect of taking months away from his beloved musical interests for prolonged analytic therapy. Freud, though himself quite unmusical, sensed Walter's needs and merely advised him to vacation in Sicily at a spa that Freud had visited and enjoyed. Walter did so and recovered rapidly and, apparently, completely. However, in anticipation of an important concert he was scheduled to conduct, he began to fear a return of his disability and once again consulted Freud. To Walter's immense relief, Freud once again advised a holiday and told him that he (Freud) would guarantee Walter's cure and success. The relief from stress and the unequivocal reassurances backed by Freud's prestige were quite effective; Walter never again felt the need to consult a psychiatrist and, despite the "superficiality" of Freud's therapy, subsequently remained relatively happy and certainly surpassingly creative.

CASE 23 Psychophysiologic Reactions of Special Sense—Amaurosis

An adolescent girl with intense sexual curiosity contrived, while unobserved, to witness intercourse between her parents. When she was discovered she developed intense guilts and fears and began to suffer attacks of functional blindness (hysterical amaurosis), as though in denial of, and expiation for, her forbidden act.

CASE 24 Psychophysiologic Musculoskeletal Reaction (Hystero-epilepsy)

Another case of sensorimotor neurosis was that of a youth of sixteen with a covertly erotic attachment to an older sister. Unable to express his incestuous fantasies in any other way, he manifested them in "epileptoid convulsions," in which the muscular movements were almost unmistakably mastur-batory or heterosexually erotic in character.

Simple explanations, reassurances and suggestions were therapeutically effective in both these instances.

## CASE 25   Hysterical Paralysis

A thirty-eight-year-old mechanic was referred by his employer, a local steel company, for a persistent weakness of the neck not explicable on a physical or neurological basis.

The history revealed that the patient, a Scandinavian émigré, had had the equivalent of only six grades of schooling and had begun to work for his present employer as a common laborer soon after his arrival in this country at the age of sixteen. He was steady and reliable but showed no special abilities; accordingly, he never progressed beyond assignments to manual labor and, in the Depression of 1930, was laid off. Unable to find another job, he retired to a small cottage in the North Woods and supported himself by gardening, fishing, and trapping as his parents had done in Lapland. In 1942, however, he was summoned back to the war-expanded plant, and, because of his previous experience, he was given a supervisory job actually beyond his intellectual and administrative capacities. He tried to hide his inefficiency by hard work over long hours, but he felt harrassed, inadequate, and increasingly tense and confused. This also served to make him "accident-prone" by repeatedly getting him into actual physical danger. One day while he was particularly resentful of his situation, he escaped having his head crushed only by the presence of mind of a fellow employee who jerked him away from a falling cable. The patient suffered a slightly sprained neck, for which, unfortunately, the local doctor prescribed an impressive-looking metal and leather supporting collar and a week's rest from work. At the end of this period the collar was removed, and recheck physical, neurologic, and x-ray examinations showed completely normal findings; however, the patient insisted that the collar be replaced. This was done for another two-week period, during which it was noted that the patient rarely rested even his chin on its padded supports; yet when the collar was again removed, the patient could not hold his head erect. Moreover, he began to complain that he suffered from general fatigue, "nervousness," muscular weakness, and sexual impotence. At the time of his referral two months later the patient was still receiving full disability compensation from his employers, was wearing his collar (although it was laced loosely with elastic and gave no cervical support), and was being cared for by his wife like a helpless child.

Psychiatric interviews by the ordinary techniques revealed few significant data other than the above, but the patient's rather naïve dreams and his direct associations showed clearly that his "paralysis" signified a surrender of masculine potency and self-sufficiency and that the collar symbolized "support"—literally, care and protection—by parent-surrogates in the form of his employers, his physicians, and his wife. The patient, therefore, unconsciously clung to his weakness and dependence as his way of acquiring greater security in what he deemed to be a frustrating and dangerous world. The techniques of treatment were attuned to these reactions. At the instance of the therapist, tactful but firm and well-coordinated pressures of his wife, company physician, and insurance company removed the secondary gains of his illness, and his employer's offer of a more suitable job at no loss in pay mitigated his occupational conflicts and mobilized a desire to return to the manual work, status, and companions that had formerly been his sources of prestige and safety. In this more favorable setting, simple insight combined with a few face-saving doses of placebo and neck massage produced a rapid and lasting recovery.

CASE 26 Psychophysiologic Musculoskeletal Reaction—Monoplegia

A twenty-two-year-old married woman, of normal intelligence but limited educational background, was referred by an obstetrician because, for a year after the delivery of a stillborn baby complicated by a mild puerperal thrombophlebitis of the right leg, she had continued to have an inexplicable spastic paralysis of this extremity. The psychiatric history was relatively specific. At the age of eighteen she had married her illiterate, stolid, but hardworking and devoted husband, mainly because she desired to escape from the drudgery of factory work. Instead of enjoying her anticipated freedom, however, she had been obliged to assume the unexpected responsibilities of a wife and prospective mother. Her first child, delivered with difficulty a year later, was born deformed, and its care added greatly to her burdens and disillusionments. Within a few months, much against her unspoken desires, she was pregnant again; this time she had an even more stormy pregnancy terminated by stillbirth and a residual thrombophlebitis. In treatment for the latter complication, the obstetrician prescribed rest, warm packs, light massage, and—psychologically most important to the patient—a suspension of intercourse until she was "completely recovered." Her husband, of course, was informed of this, and remained continent for months, although finally his growing impatience forced the patient again to seek treatment for what she called, with significant lack of anxiety, her "chronic milk leg."[1] In the psychiatric interview the patient quite innocently stated that there were certain things about her leg she "couldn't understand," e.g., why it was "better" throughout the day, yet so painfully stiff in adduction at night that intercourse with her husband was impossible. Fortunately, the symptom cleared rapidly when the patient recognized its relationship to her fears of a third pregnancy, although her self-respect and rapport were preserved by making this point implicit, but never traumatizingly explicit. Furthermore, since insight without action never solves a dilemma, the therapy was directly implemented by inducing her husband, through appeals to his own self-interest, to practice the contraceptive techniques that, with their priest's permission, they both really desired.

## THERAPY OF PSYCHOSOMATIC DISORDERS

Fortunately, since most psychologic counselors are sympathetic and dedicated human beings, they function *intuitively* well, in the sense that from early youth every civilized person has "learned inwardly" how to deal with those who appeal to him for comfort and solace, else he himself would have become a pariah. To implement this general empathy, the psychotherapist's further education should be designed to lead out (Latin: *e-duce*) and develop special capacities and skills with which to relieve the triune physical, social and philosophic tribulations (Ur-anxieties) of his fellowman. He will then act in three capacities.

---

[1] This understandable lack of concern about a symptomatic disability that serves to resolve a neurotic conflict was called *la belle indifference* by Janet. Clinically, however, anxiety can be readily elicited if the symptom is prematurely threatened by the therapist.

First, the therapist endeavors *to alleviate pain and fear*. Here the physician has an opportunity granted to no other mortals: to relieve primal anxiety by using his knowledge and skill to heal physical disease and postpone death; therefore medical and surgical procedures are often an indispensable part of "psycho" therapy. For example, the first step in treating the mental as well as the physical desuetude that accompanies some forms of anemia is to administer iron, Vitamin $B_{12}$, or other hemopoietic medication. The most effective available relief for the sword-of-Damocles anxiety and overreactive assertiveness that characterize an epileptic, or the defensive retreat and regressive dependency of those afflicted with neuromuscular disease, is the proper antiepileptic or tremor-relieving medication. So also, gastric or duodenal ulcers should never be treated by "emotional insight" alone, since antacids and antispasmodics are equally necessary to break the psychosomatic cycle. Judicious prescription of *nonspecific drugs* may likewise be useful. An agitated, distracted melancholic may listen to reason much more readily after a night or two of restful sleep induced by simple sedatives; a patient in a state of exhausted lethargy may be helped back to responsiveness by properly used stimulants. However, two all-important cautions must be observed: First, sedative (sitting) or hypnotic (sleeping) medications must be used only for temporary relief, while more basic life readjustments are being worked through; and second, all drugs must be prescribed *with proper safeguards* when the patient is inclined to escape realities either by cultivating addiction to the drug employed (or to a substitute almost everywhere available—alcohol) or by using it for suicidal gestures.

Second, the therapist must help *rebuild the patient's social confidence*. Whether he admits it consciously or not, the patient comes to the therapist much as a hurt and frightened child appeals to his parents for instant, individual, devoted, and seemingly unselfish care, and as an ally against a disappointing or hostile world. It is therefore essential to learn whether familial, economic, cultural, or other life stresses have preceded, and presumably contributed to, the patient's symptoms. This can be done briefly and tactfully by using common euphemisms, such as inquiries about "overwork," "worry about the family," or "business troubles," that the patient will accept as proper medical concern rather than invasions of privacy. A few minutes spent in such a survey will often reveal direct relationships between intercurrent life stresses and easily recognizable psychiatric syndromes, and thereby spare both the doctor and the patient prolonged, fruitless organic searching, and misdirected therapy.

Unless there are definite reasons to the contrary (e.g., in homosexual, seductive, paranoiac, or delusional patients) a physician's professional concern may be further signified by at least a partial physical examination, if for no other reason than that the mother's pat, the king's touch, and the prophet's laying on of hands have always been effective in promoting what is discerningly called reciprocal "good feeling."

Once begun, the physician must continue this personalized care of the patient without ever delegating it wholly to others until the patient no longer needs him in this central role. This includes acting as his special Vergil during hospitalizations, operations, and convalescence, since this personal relationship may be the most important single instrument in restoring his trust in humanity and in recultivating other interests, companions, and friends. If he needs more prolonged and intensive psychiatric care, the therapist can best persuade him to seek it or to enter a mental hospital—after which the therapist may resume his role as a guide to the world outside.

Finally, the therapist can *help restore the patient's faith in a universal order*. Although in our culture it is customary to distinguish "worldly" from "spiritual" responsibilities, the broadly humanitarian practitioner should not be blind to his patients' needs for transcendental beliefs and "spiritual" comfort. The therapist should therefore maintain no prejudices about collaborating with the minister, rabbi, or priest in restoring to the patient a sense of cosmic belonging and divine as well as mundane protection, incidentally earning reciprocal respect and cooperation from men of the cloth.

Effective implementation of these objectives in therapy has sometimes been compared to a game of chess: The principles governing the opening and closing moves can be fairly clearly stated, but the maneuvers in between must ever be determined by the talent, insight, and forethought of each player in dealing with an individual situation. Accordingly, there are no rules that will guarantee success in every or even any instance, but these generalizations may be helpful:

No patient should be labeled with a one- or two-word "diagnosis"; such nosology is no longer taken as adequately meaningful by experienced psychiatrists. Instead, the therapist must try to understand the nature of the patient's desires and tribulations, the effective (*normal*), deviant (*neurotic*), or bizarrely unrealistic (*psychotic*) ways he tries to deal with them, and the relative accessibility of these patterns of behavior to the therapeutic influences outlined. Explanations in pseudoanalytic clichés such as "oral fixations," "Oedipus complex," "latent homosexuality," etc., should also be avoided: Such obsolescent epithets may vent covert dislike of the patient, but they furnish no leads to dynamic aid. In general, brief, direct, and effective therapy concentrates on the patient's *real* and *present* problems and their practical solutions. It is true that the patient's conduct has evolved from his previous life experiences, but those cannot be relived and altered; instead the patient's *reactions* to his past should be explored and evaluated only to clarify his current misconceptions. Once again, *all therapeutic reeducation consists of abandoning patterns that are no longer adequate and exploring and adopting new ones that are more personally and socially profitable.*

The patient's confidences are, of course, never violated; but this does not exclude conferences with—or even the concurrent psychotherapy of—his friends, family, employer, or other persons who may be contributing to or sharing his neurosis. Rarely, however, should the therapist furnish arbitrary directions as to major changes such as the selection of a career, conception or adoption of a child, initiation or stopping a divorce action, etc. If the patient is helped to see clearly the alternatives and consequences of his behavior, he will not need such advice; if he follows it blindly, dubiously, or resentfully, his actions are quite likely to circumvent or vitiate its intent—and the therapist will, quite justifiably, be blamed for the results.

## The Later Years

The procedures outlined above apply generally to the therapy not only of "psychosomatic disorders" but to most of the underlying personality problems of adult life.

CASE 27 Conversion Reaction in an Infantile Personality

An attractive, intelligent thirty-year-old spinster applied to the university clinics with a single complaint of a slight paresthesia or weakness of the left arm since she had begun work as a comptometer operator a month previously. On further enquiry the patient could recollect only a few other symptoms: occasional "dizzy spells," mild phobias, and a tendency to social shyness. The patient agreed with her most recent physician in attributing all of these symptoms to "nervousness," although she apparently regarded the latter as a type of disease *sui generis* "affecting her nervous system," which required proper rest, diet, and medication.

In contrast with the seeming mildness of the presenting illness stood the patient's past history. This revealed feeding difficulties, night terrors and other neurotic aberrations in early childhood, marked dependence on the mother and rivalry with her younger brother, persistent enuresis until the age of thirteen, disciplinary troubles at school with frequent absenteeism for various vague illnesses, a fragmentary evolution of interests in social and recreational outlets, and diffuse phobias and inhibitions with reactions of anxiety under circumstances of even mild sexual or social stress. There was almost no emancipation from the family in adolescence; in fact, the dependence on her mother—an aggressive, preemptive woman —continued to be so intense that the patient still lived, ate, and slept with her, and could hardly bear a day's separation.

As to her "medical" history, the patient had been consulting a long succession of doctors for various complaints since childhood and had received a vast variety of treatments, including naturopathic diets, chiropractic adjustments, and endocrine therapy. When the patient was 16 her parents separated and sued for divorce; concurrently she developed episodes of weakness, trembling, and fatigue. A thyroidectomy was advised and performed, but the patient's symptoms showed no marked improvement until the divorce was settled, and she was able to return to her mother. Nevertheless, the patient continued her attendance at various clinics, eagerly accepted each new diagnosis, and cooperated passively with whatever was prescribed. This practice was apparently encouraged by the mother who, by keeping the patient "ill" and ostensibly in need of constant care, forestalled any possible emancipation from maternal dominance. Another effect of this relationship was the patient's inadaptability at work, as shown by the fact that since her graduation from high school at 18 she had held four jobs an average of two months and had quit each of them to "rest" or undergo various new "treatment" for her long succession of illnesses.

Finally, the symptoms that occasioned her admission to the clinics developed when she had been forced by financial needs to work as a comptometrist in a large office. She had taken an instant dislike to her routine mechanical duties, which, indeed, were considerably below her intellectual capacities. At about the same time, her younger brother arrived home on an army furlough and, being a hero in uniform, temporarily displaced the patient from her accustomed position as the center of family attention. In reaction, the patient developed diffuse anxiety and the "conversion" symptom of an arm paralysis, which simultaneously denied her jealous aggressions, made work impossible, and justified a return to infantile dependence. Indeed, she achieved the regressive gain of admission to a private room, doctors' and nurses' attention, and the renewed concern of her mother, who hovered over her almost constantly at the hospital. True, these advantages were obtained at the cost of certain sacrifices, such as temporary surrender of freedom and activity, but the patient's relative lack of alarm over her symptoms and her cheerfully self-prescribed course of treatment demonstrated clearly that her "disabilities" were far from unacceptable. On the contrary, as indicated by the survey of her past history, they were simply another expression of fixed patterns of infantile dependency, covertly homosexual maternal fixations, and other neurotic defenses that had characterized her behavior since childhood.

COURSE

The patient's rapid but unstable symptomatic "improvement" under therapy and her profession of enthusiastic but essentially spurious "insight" into her difficulties also proved instructive. As she once again formed a childishly dependent relationship to her physicians her anxiety rapidly abated, after which she avidly "accepted" their explanations and assurances that her paralysis had no organic basis and could be readily overcome by appropriate understanding and effort on her part. Direct suggestions combined with the prescription of arm exercises and occupational therapy readily restored complete function to the arm, and within a week the patient declared herself symptom-free. In the same way she followed the doctors' leads in discussing her excessive devotion to her mother, her jealousies of her father and her brother, her feelings of personal inferiority, and her anxieties with regard to past and current familial, sexual, social, and occupational problems. She likewise volunteered data to the effect that many of her previous "illnesses" as well as her "nervous breakdowns" had been precipitated by conflicts over these problems. Moreover, she admitted that any lasting recovery would entail serious attempts on her part to achieve familial emancipation, stable occupational adjustments, and the development of satisfactory extrafamilial interests and social relationships.

Two weeks after her admission, the patient was discharged from the hospital relieved of her symptoms, professing complete "insight," and apparently intent upon sweeping changes in her ways of living. And yet, the poor prognosis indicated by her past performances was entirely justified by a follow-up study of her case two years later. At that time it was learned that two days after her discharge from the hospital, the patient had "accidentally" slipped down a short flight of stairs at the first place she applied for a position and immediately had developed back pains and "weakness of the legs."

Neurologists and orthopedic physicians who were called into consultation could find no evidence of physical injury; nevertheless, the patient spent the next month once again recuperating under her mother's tender care. At the end of this period, anorexia and other mild but persistent organic dysfunctions reappeared, and the patient quickly relapsed into her accustomed rounds of chiropractors, naturopaths, doctors, and clinics.

## THE CLIMACTERIUM

However, in some individuals there are two later periods of crisis that require special consideration. The disorders of mood and behavior that occur in some women in our culture during their fifth decade of life are often attributed by them to the physical effects of the menopause, so that they can conveniently blame their concurrent erratic and troublesome behavior to a metabolic imbalance beyond their control. Indeed, so avidly do some women cling to this rationalization that for years they will go from one physician to another demanding medicines or injections of vitamins and hormones—or to nonmedical practitioners for diets, baths, exercises, or patent nostrums—to delay or reverse the dreaded "change of life." True, minute quantities of estrogens and progesterones administered in proper sequence may help relieve the "hot flashes" and "dizzy spells" (*vasomotor disturbances*), transient palpitations, and mild abdominal and muscular cramps that sometimes occur in women during the gradual cessation of menstruation, but they have no other direct physiologic effect on behavior. It has also become fashionable for some men, especially those in higher economic echelons, to blame their difficulties on a corresponding "male climacterium" and to demand therapy with pituitary or testicular extracts. However, the real reasons for most of the difficulties experienced by both sexes in later middle life—which, in the larger sense of necessary reorientations in self-evaluations, accomplishments to date, and realistic prospects, do indeed necessitate a sometimes poignantly painful "change of life"—can be summarized as follows:

FEMALE

The years between forty and fifty often present problems that some women take very seriously. On the physical side, their verve, beauty, and sexual attractiveness undeniably fade, despite all artificial aids, and no longer command flattering attentions from a husband or other men whose interests unmistakably begin to wander elsewhere. Social successes diminish, while former acquaintances pall and younger, more energetic women are elected to the chairmanship of Hadassah, the district PTA, or the annual Charity Bazaar. Worse, sons and daughters grow up, depart for school and careers, marry, and ever more frankly and firmly resent attempts at continued maternal control. All that seems to remain is a life with less and less adventure, achievement, influence, or satisfaction—a dour and depressing vista. If renewed social climbing, frenetic extramarital flirtations, martyred protests about the ingratitude of husband, children, and friends, or increasing doses of tranquilizers all prove ineffective, one recourse remains: Blame the recurrent anxieties and episodes of restless melancholy on failing glands rather than failing resources and adaptabilities and demand that the therapist—usually a physician required to act simultaneously as internist, gynecologist, father confessor, wailing wall, counselor, Platonic lover, and magician—reverse time, restore past powers and glories, and prevent inexorable senescence.

## CASE 28 Therapy of a "Menopausal Neurosis"

A forty-seven-year-old woman, after seven years of therapy by three successive psychoanalysts, was referred to me for continued alcoholism and recurrent depressive episodes; characteristically, she made an immediate dive for my office couch in the middle of our first interview. To establish what rapport I could through the only channel thus offered, I permitted her for several more sessions to ramble on supinely about her dreams, her early childhood, her intricate "object cathexes," "introjections," "transference distortions," and various other periphrastic vacuities, by which she and her former analysts had long tried to avoid dealing with the realities of her life. One day, however, she walked in with an obvious limp. When I responded to this overture by asking why, she told me that, while gardening that morning, she had stepped on a rake, one prong of which had penetrated the sole of her foot. Having gone only this far, she tried to preclude further intrusions by informing me that she herself knew that her adventure in the garden was a form of acting-out designed to cause a symbolic erection of the rake handle, and that she freely wished to admit unconscious erotic satisfaction in the penetration of the phallic prong into her downwardly displaced vaginal instep. The ensuant bleeding, of course, represented a regression to, and a reenactment of, her fantasied adolescent defloration by a "brother–father surrogate" who, because of his erotic activities, had been called "a rake" by her "castrative mother." At this point I interrupted her harangue (which only a somewhat retarded first-year analytic trainee could regard as anything but evasive and covertly derisive) with the statement that, whether or not she regarded it as neurotic voyeurism on my part, I wished to examine the wound on her foot. In shocked amazement, she complied and showed me a puncture lesion on her heel still surrounded by specks of imbedded dirt. I promptly sent my secretary for a vial of tetanus antitoxin and, after proper inquiry as to the patient's serum sensitivity, asked her to bare one buttock, informing her that, whether or not she interpreted the syringe and injection as a sexual intromission and ejaculation, no patient of mine was going to develop tetanus convulsions if I could prevent it.

That "physical" treatment, taken by the patient as evidence of my realistic concern and therapeutic competence, proved to be a crucial point in her therapy and in her life. In later interviews she abandoned her covert methods of using pseudoanalytic persiflage to frustrate analysts at their favorite one-upmanship games; instead, we both began to deal with her specific concerns about children who had grown, married, and left her, a husband who seemed only occasionally successful either in his business or in concealing his extramarital adventures, her failures to find security in a minor political career likewise seasoned with a sexual liaison, her dread of losing the rest of her fading attractiveness, and other such actual or fancied stresses. Within three months she found new satisfactions in greatly improved relations with her children, husband, and lover, in being elected president of her state PTA, and in other achievements that rendered her alcoholism or punitive depressions no longer necessary.

MALE

It can now be seen why men also cherish the alibi of an organic change, since at the same ages many in our culture must also undergo, to use a hackneyed but appropriate phrase, quite agonizing reappraisals of their past, present, and future. Advancing decrepitude of physique becomes undeniable, and sexual prowess—equated by many with general strength and virility—also begins to fail under the demands of increasingly frantic testing. Occupational and social limitations must likewise be faced: Unrealistic ambitions must be given up and efforts bent to the humiliating task of retaining one's present position against younger, better-prepared competitors. Friends on whom one relied for help may have escalated out of reach or are faring worse than oneself—and in the latter case become awkward liabilities. The wife and children have become disillusioned, and either complain openly of their disappointments or assume a martyred, maddeningly patronizing air toward "poor "Dad" who "tried hard and meant well, so we'll try not to say anything to hurt his feelings." In short, life has not fulfilled the conifident expectations of youth and early manhood—and ahead lies nothing but increasingly bleak and lonesome old age. Perhaps—just perhaps—all this can still be changed by the concentrated vigor contained in the proper vitamin or hormone pill, or a dose of renewed masculinity injected through a syringe; the aging gladiator fervently hopes that some physician—or goat gland engrafter, naturopath, chiropractor, or other necromancer—can cure the temporary gonadal imbalance involved. If that is not the case, then some Hubbardian "scientologist," Buchmanite faith healer, Christian Scientist, or T-group leader can clear his Conscious, dissipate his Suppressed Complexes, correct the errors of Thought, release and ultilize latent Sensitivities and Potencies, and so bring about a Physical Rebirth and an Emotional Enlightment that will dispel the gathering evening shadows. But faith does not always spring eternal to counter melancholy; and presenile rage, disorganization, and decay may ensue. The therapist must therefore proceed with empathy and wisdom.

If necessary to establish rapport, drugs may be administered, not only for their reassuring (Latin: *place-bo* "I wish to please") effect, but also to ease actual menopausal symptoms when present in women, and to alleviate excessive tension and to induce interim relaxation and sleep in both sexes. However, it must be clearly understood that this is their limited function, else disappointments and loss of confidence will occur when permanent relief is not obtained.

Once the patient has achieved some symptomatic relief, and rapport has been gained, tactful, perceptive inquiry will, as noted, nearly always elicit an illuminating account of his anxieties, doubts, fears, and perplexities, accompanied by appeals for sympathy, advice, and, not infrequently, personal service sometimes extending beyond strict professional limits. Perceptive empathy rather than sympathy (which some patients take to mean that they have, after all, always been right and the world always wrong) may be tendered; however, indulgent partisanships and personal interference should be avoided as generally leading to complications for all concerned, and guidance given only in the sense of helping the patient reorder his life according to a simple truism: *Improve what can yet be changed and make the best of the rest.*

*Reorientation.* Rut-formed patterns can still be altered to possible advantage: Goals can be modified, old interests and friendships renewed, fresh ones cultivated, and broader horizons of life explored. Care must be taken, however, to conserve what is fundamentally valuable in the patient's life; only rarely will a defiant resignation, an impulsive move to a strange environment, a late shuffling of marital partners, or other such major changes solve more problems than they evoke.

*Adaptation.* Readjustments must be made in accordance with another ancient aphorism: Happiness is not a simple summation of material or interpersonal possessions or guarantees but the *ratio between what is possessed and what is desired.* In effect, if the patient will but scale down his demands to approximately what is available, contentment is obviously within reach. In appearance, a woman can regard her gray-streaked hair as "maturely becoming" and a man his bald pate as distinguished as Caesar's or Eisenhower's. Athletically, one set of tennis doubles or a leisurely nine holes of golf—or for that matter a quiet afternoon sail or even a game of shuffleboard—can be enjoyed almost as thoroughly as three sets of singles, water-skiing, or ice-boating used to be. Sexual intercourse once every week or two may furnish more satisfying orgasms than partial impotence or premature ejaculations experienced in more frequent attempts at coitus. Socioeconomically, the position of accountant, shop foreman, rewrite man, or associate professor may, on rational reflection, be considered as actually more secure and comfortable than those of chief auditor, company president, city editor, or departmental chairman; and interpersonally, the devotion of spouse, children, and grandchildren can still be earned rather than demanded, provided possessiveness and exploitation are no longer considered one's due. These reevaluations may at first be rejected by the patient as an unconscionable surrender of his or her cherished ambitions and rightful expectations, but careful and repeated review of alternatives generally leads to a reasonable resolution of the patient's physical, social, and philosophic difficulties, gratitude to the therapist, and perhaps of most importance, avoidance of even more poignant difficulties in later years.

## Problems of Aging

Our animal cousins, like ourselves, treat their aged according to the needs of their social order. Ruminants such as the red deer cherish and protect elderly cows and bucks, since experienced survivors can lead the herd to remote trails and pasturages unknown to the young. In contrast, predatory wolves exile their aged to fend for themselves after they can no longer earn their share of the pack's kill. In human parallels, good gray Homer was revered in Hellenic times as a sage and a poet, and in republican Rome the Seniors of the city governed in the Senate. So, also, in the peaceful and aesthetic Finnish Golden Era (as idealized in the Kalevala mythology) the elderly were romantically cherished because they knew the songs and sagas that recounted the grace and glory of their ancient race. In stark contrast, if the communal food supply became insufficient among the Labrador Eskimos during a particularly hard winter, the patriarch was expected to leave the village and quietly freeze to death—yet, since the eldest son accompanied him part way on this last journey to bid him farewell, the oldster felt that he was still an honored member of his family and community and would, therefore, in a wishful fantasy immanent in all of us, be rewarded in some more pleasant land beyond.

Our discussions of etiology at various times of life have been so phrased as to relate them to experiences everyone in our culture is almost certain to have had: the dependencies of childhood; the adventures and rebellions of youth; the economic, sexual, and cultural adaptations of adulthood; and the reorientations and re-castings of late middle age. In the same way we can understand, again through personal experience, the oppressive *anxieties* of the neurotic when his individually cultivated physical, social, or philosophic techniques are faced with failure, his spreading avoid-ances (*phobias*) of times, places, and situations that symbolize this threat, or his ritualized thinking (*obsessions*) and maneuvers (*com-pulsions*) with which he tries, in part realistically and in part magically, to regain control. With regard to delirious reactions, most of us have had acute illnesses, with accompanying temporary cripplings and transient confusions before an eventual return to reasonable physical strength, intellectual clarity, and renewed com-petence. So, also, on deeper probing our experience does not fail us in empathizing even with those we call *psychotic:* When pressed down (*de-pressed*) too greatly by adversities, we have all at times suffered from loss of sleep, energy, and appetite, become dolorous, bitter, demanding of sympathy and helplessly dependent—and hence we have all had episodes of *melancholia.* Or we may have tried to rationalize our failures and aggrandize our status by attributing all our difficulties to the nefarious plots of important and influential enemies diabolically organized to frustrate our genius—and have thus taken an occasional step toward *paranoia.* As to even more bizarre aberrations of thought and conduct, in our fantasies and dreams we have also felt ourselves independent of time, place, restraint, or logic, masters of strange realities in stranger sequences, and immersed in emotions incompatible with civilized living—hence we differ from a *schizophrenic* only in being somewhat less continuously divorced from "reality." Here, however, is the rub: In contrast to all such experiences, none of us will admit to having been irreversibly and hopelessly *senile,* and therefore we find it most difficult to reconstruct from our own experiences what the elderly must feel. Instead, our concepts of the role and treatment of the aged are secondarily indoctrinated and have varied greatly with time and culture.

In our modern American society, the epitome of the acceptable senior citizen—who at age sixty-five or over will soon constitute a fourth of the population—is, on the whole, significantly different from the examples cited, though it borrows subtle components from all of them. Thus, the typically successful "retired American" is generally pictured in our advertising arts as a well-to-do and peripatetic playboy. His wife, to paraphrase a Western song, is not dowdy or gray—she is an attractive platinum blonde not averse to displaying a remarkably well-preserved figure. The two of them—provided, of course, they subscribed in time to Social Security, Medicare, and the largesse of the Rugged Individualist Retirement Insurance Company—can spend their Independent Golden Years fishing, golfing, or yachting with retained tan and vigor anywhere from the Azure Coast of California to the Verdant Virgin Islands. The Cornell Study by Street and Thompson of some 2,000 older people indicated that five-sixths of those in the upper economic brackets who can achieve a reasonable facsimile of this economic goal can indeed remain relatively content; regrettably, most Americans cannot. Instead, whereas in 1910 there were ten workers who remained at their jobs throughout their lives to every one who "retired," the proportion now is only four to one, and it is estimated that by 1975 there will be thirty million idle people over sixty-five in our country, many living pathetically on local or federal subsidies.

It is against this background of physical and socioeconomic realities that the "psychodynamics of aging" can best be understood. One cannot make a complete distinction between the actual disabilities of the senium (i.e., diminished ability to perceive, differentiate, abstract, and evaluate the environment, and to respond in a properly versatile and efficient fashion) and the reactions of the individual aged person to such impairments of capacity and opportunity. Not only the declining artist and the impaired intellectual but every person in every walk of life becomes embittered by, and attempts to compensate for, failing powers and threatened status by reactions that appear in any chronic debilitating process. For example, as Ferenczi and Hollos demonstrated, the paranoid grandiosity of paresis (cerebral syphilis) is not due to the disease itself but is a function of the patient's responses to the unconsciously sensed threat to his health, social securities, and rational intregity. In normal aging, there is a corresponding intensification of these basic Ur-defenses of the personality. Physically, the presenile tries strenuously to reassert his waning vigor in various activities from gardening through golf to gynecophilia; socially, he clings avidly to whatever human relationships remain available to him; and psychologically, he adopts and ardently defends philosophic or religious systems that deny death and promise some form of immortal existence and power.

GERIATRIC THERAPY

PREVENTIVE MEASURES

Economic factors aside, to avert the empty isolation of old age one must develop, while still young, a versatility of interests, techniques, and satisfactions that can be continued throughout life. Literature, music, art, philosophy—these are perennial joys, and almost independent of retained manipulative skills. Broad experience in itself may also become a commodity the marketability of which does not depreciate: The ancient mariner who loves the seas and still knows the proper rig and trim of a ship invites the respect and company of sailors of all ages. Nevertheless, without undue cynicism it can also be said that a certain rugged expectation of and tolerance for disappointment and even injustice is another asset to be acquired long before the senium in this not quite perfect world.

## PSYCHOTHERAPY

Perhaps the first consideration is to apply the Golden Rule and grant our elders beliefs and practices that we ourselves will eventually cherish. If dear old Uncle Harry thinks that yoga or yogurt will make him a virile centenarian or if aging Aunt Harriet believes that she still looks enticing in a bikini, why, then, such foibles up to the point of inviting social derision may be charitably condoned as relatively harmless. With regard to avidity for cants and cults, let us remember that even great men in their last years professed some fairly odd philosophies: the sociologist Auguste Comte literally worshipped his dead wife Clothilde as Queen of the Heavenly Society; the cosmologist Arthur Eddington began to believe that God, too, was but a fellow-mathematician; Sir Oliver Lodge became an ardent Spiritualist; and Sigmund Freud himself, facing his fatal cancer, symbolically mastered it by including an "instinct for death itself" (*Thanatos*) in his supposedly deathless metapsychology.

However, wishful fantasies and self-aggrandizements are not enough; maintained social contacts and controls are also necessary. If these are not furnished along constructive channels, the aged may retreat to querulous dependencies and in a sense demand indulgent baby-sitters for their second childhood. In contrast, if they are given continued opportunities to exercise their remaining occupational and social skills, the cycle of familial disruption and parasitism may be long postponed.

CASE 29 Rehabilitation in Later Life

A seventy-two-year-old patient, before his retirement, had been very successful as the owner of a string of cigar factories. After half a decade of idleness or aimless travel, he had begun to drink, gamble, and—perhaps with not altogether unconscious intent—"disgrace" his children with various escapades until, by legal threats, they forced him to seek treatment. The therapist abjured the role of parole officer, actively cultivated the patient's confidence, and professed genuine interest in the social implications of the patient's "pioneer contributions to American industry"—particularly as to how he had eliminated marginal labor by substituting machines for cigar-rolling Puerto Ricans. This encouraged the patient to regale the therapist with instructive lectures on industry and commerce, during which he evolved a plan for starting a string of little tobacco counters in downtown buildings that were to feature the products of the various factories that still bore his name. Once he started on this project, and almost until his death eight years later, he was a sometimes forgetful and fretful, but mostly alert, active, reasonably self-restrained, certainly quite likeable, and undoubtedly happier old man.

As may now be inferred, the therapy of the elderly is, whenever possible, best conducted where they can retain, at least in part, their place as senior citizens still valued by their community. Indeed, this attitude appears also in the unique filial *transference-countertransference relationships* necessary in geriatric psychotherapy, in that the aged like to picture the therapist or social worker not as a loved or feared parent-figure, but as a dutiful son or daughter properly devoted to their interests. But members of a family do not question, let alone imprison, their elders; instead, they visit them at home, bringing presents, and are rewarded by advice and benedictions—hence the many advantages of tactfully arranged home care plans as opposed to even the most aseptic and best-conducted "Hospitals for the Incurable Aged."

INSTITUTIONAL CARE

However, if this becomes necessary, the objectives must be

changed from total custody to provisions for relieving the family and the community of the most burdensome aspects of caring for their aged member only when necessary. The family can be assured that during episodes of illness, or even if they simply want a vacation, they will have some place to leave the oldsters. This relief can range from two or three hours a day through a day or two a week to total in-patient care for several months—but never with the intent of "terminal commitment." By this means the community's conscience is neither overstrained nor lulled, whereas the family, under this combined surveillance and succorance, resumes its lightened but remaining obligations.

Institutions for the aged should be organized along special lines. There must be a diagnostic unit in which the internist, psychiatrist, psychologist, and social worker collaborate in clarifying and modifying favorably the medical, psychodynamic, and social factors in the patient's behavior. According to British statistics (Z. Cosin *et al.*), nine out of ten of the hospitalized aged, if given appropriate medical care, can be returned within two or three weeks to their families, sufficiently free of the metabolic, circulatory, or toxic-delirious reactions that had been mistaken for senile deterioration. Patients who must remain longer are sent to a continuous treatment unit and then to a rehabilitation section or— as necessary in remarkably few cases—to a small ward where chronic bedfast patients are kept. It is the day hospital, however, that is the most important aspect of an effective modern institution. Here are provisions for physiotherapy, occupational therapy, and for transporting the patient at optimal intervals to the hospital and back to his family. The goal is, indeed, almost the minimum number of inactive hours: Even if the patients are doing nothing better than whittling and sanding tongue depressors out of old orange crates, they are proudly accomplishing something useful. Hours of idleness or unsupervised "group discussion" are avoided, since they become no more than periods of boredom, spite, and squabble. There is also a night hospital (without the necessity of a doctor or a nurse in residence) for those who can be maintained at outside work and simply come in in the evening and stay overnight. Finally, there are group day and/or night units of eight or nine rooms where an *esprit de corps* is built around one meal a day and various group activities. Here the old people generally run the organization and live as a little community with minimal protection and provisions by the state. All in all, such geriatric clinics and hospitals will differ markedly from the huge custodial institutions we are still tolerating in this country. They will require fewer dollars, but more medical attention, intelligent social work, and a great deal of familial reorientations and community education—and therapeutic competence of a higher order.

# Past, Present, and Future

It had formerly seemed logical, and has therefore become customary, to begin the exposition of a subject with a review of its history before scrutinizing its current status or predicting its future. Yet this is not necessarily the best sequence, since it can dissipate or vitiate an interest that would otherwise have been intensified by direct and vivid dealing with current material. For example, the evolution of violin-making is fascinating reading only to those who have already learned to play and love the instrument, since history relates not only how this stringed wonder came to be, but how the lute, viola, cello, double bass, and other of its preceding forms also became useful in the orchestra. Accordingly, in this section of the book we shall trace in historical perspective various aspects of psychiatry, and thus perhaps be better able to understand the rationale, goals, and techniques of current modes of therapy.

## Biodynamic Roots of the Ur-Defenses

Three billion years ago in the Algonkian slime where DNA came into being, life itself was characterized by two essential properties: first, a capacity to maintain its integrity by manipulating with ever-greater efficiency its circumambient milieu; and second, an intrinsic tendency toward interorganismic collaboration. As part of the latter heritage, a modern myxamoeba, which still survives as little else but a blob of DNA- and RNA-organized protoplasm, remains a rugged individualist, providing everything is going relatively well; however, should its environment dry up or food become scarce, it will congregate with others to form a *clone* in which some cells die so that others can feed, sporulate, and survive. Somewhat higher in the scale of evolution, it is difficult for a biologist to determine whether a Portuguese man-of-war can be regarded biologically as a fortuitous collection of individuals, a cooperative colony, or a unitary, complex animal.

To skip countless aeons of animate evolution, fifty thousand years ago men had the brain potential and all of the physical endowments we have today, plus their stone axes, scrapers, throwing darts, and a growing arsenal of tools with which to better manipulate their milieu. Concurrently, they had joined in common endeavors with apportioned roles and organization; significantly also, they had developed a system of beliefs in a universal order that could at least in part be controlled by earthly fetishes and rituals. For example, they carved mammiferous and obese amulets, now called paleolithic Venuses, which magically invoked the eternal comforts of the deified Wife and Mother. Their cave paintings at Altamira in Spain and Lascaux in France depicted not only the weapons and prowess of individuals and their collaboration in the tribal hunt, but also were placed in alcoves very much like primitive chapels, were surrounded by articles of religious ritual and apparently epitomized man's dreams and hopes in the sense that by the poetry of his imagination he could control his fate here and hereafter. In effect, the basic assumptions and maneuvers by which men always sought to mitigate uncertainty and bolster security—and which we now employ in what we call psychotherapy—had already been evolved in human prehistory.

In the much more explicitly documented practices in the Asklepiad Sanatoria of Greece and Rome (named after the son of Apollo, god of music, mind, and medicine), the therapeutic techniques employed were more elaborately developed as follows:

RESTORATION OF PHYSICAL WELL-BEING

After the patient had left his contentious home and traveled to one of the Sanatoria in the salubrious environs of Cos, Memphis, or Knidos, he was met not by a clerk or social worker, but by no less a parent-surrogate than the Head Priest or Priestess, who welcomed him and instilled an expectation of recovery by conducting him past piles of discarded crutches and bronze plaques bearing testimonials from grateful ex-patients. Attention was then concentrated on restoring the applicant's zest and vigor through rest in pleasant surroundings, nourishing and appetizing diets, relaxing baths and massages, and the carefully measured administration of nepenthics—drugs that resembled modern tranquilizers in that they apparently soothed both the patient and the doctor.

RECULTIVATION OF HUMAN RELATIONSHIPS

With this objective, equal effort was expended in counteracting social alienation by *developing confidence in the physician.* Then, as now, the sufferer was encouraged to relate to his therapist:

1.  As a kindly and protective parental figure who provided a source of security and comfort.
2.  As a learned and experienced teacher, whose counsels for more restrained and balanced and therefore healthier and happier modes of life could be followed on rational and practical grounds (e.g., as in the various Stoic schools).

3.  As a personal mentor uniquely interested in the supplicant's complaints and difficulties ("present illness") and willing to explore their relationship to his past experiences (*psychiatric history*), their meanings and values (*symbolisms*), and acquired patterns of goal-directed action (*operational analysis*), in order that the verbal understandings so derived would lead to more satisfying, lasting, and useful adaptations (*operational insight*). Socrates required his students to think through their own verbal perplexities, and Plato understood the unconscious significance of dreams and symbols. Aristophanes, in his delightful comedy *The Clouds,* pictured the distraught Strepsiades being placed by Socrates on a couch and learning through "free-associations" that his fantasy of controlling the phases of the moon meant that he didn't want to pay his monthly bills. As noted, Soranus records the cure of a case of "hysteria" in a virginal bride by a form of direct uxorial action that would shock a modern sexologist.

4.  The physician's prestige led to an avid faith in the efficacy of his quasi-scientific, quasi-mystical remedies. The arsenal of the Hellenic practitioner included not only medicaments from Cathay to the Gates of Hercules but also a vast variety of surgical and other manipulations available for the treatment of the weak or ailing, such as the Egyptian practice of trephining the skull and incising the cortex (*lobotomy*) or, as described by Pliny the Elder, by subjecting the patient to *convulsive therapy* by discharging electric eels through his head. We read of Hippocrates' condemnations of the "ignorrance and superstition inherent in many of these false remedies," but this alone proves how widely practiced, then as now, they must have been.

In addition, the Sanatoria also cultivated group activities that included the following modalities:

1.  Music, which provided aesthetic expression and encouraged

group belongingness through feelings of conjoint rhythm and harmony.

2.  Calisthenics and dancing, which afforded similar possibilities of reassuring interpersonal contacts.
3.  Competitive athletics, not only for the joy of restorative exercise but for public recognition through nondestructive competition and reward.
4.  Dramatics, in which basic human relationships were more deeply explored in the plays of Euripides, Aeschylus, or Aristophanes, offering the patient, either as witness or participant, vivid identifications and vicarious representations of his own interpersonal problems.[1] The Greeks cherished and utilized these tragedies and comedies for their deep human empathy and ageless significance, endlessly varied their themes, and were personally involved as actors, chorus, or affectively moved audience—and thus anticipated modern forms of *psychodrama*.
5.  Social rehabilitation, which offered a transition between a passive dependence on the sanatorium to an eventual recognition of the advantage of a return to the community and service for the common good.

The Sanatoria tried, finally, to encourage an Ur-illusion of transcendent order. Because of the eternal necessity of this last belief, even the sophisticated Greeks demanded that Socrates pay the ultimate penalty for threatening man's trust in the existence of beneficent celestial Beings. To capitalize on this ultimate faith, the Asklepiad Sanatoria, like many hospitals today, were built and operated by one or another religious order, which added powerful factors to therapy: a "divinely revealed" doctrine in which all who wished to believe could feel an exclusively self-elevating bond of

---

[1] See discussion of the Oedipus trilogy, p. 75.

mystical fellowship; and a reassuring ritual that, through its origin in human needs and through millennia of empiric refinement, included exquisitely gratifying procedures such as:

1.  The symbolic eating and drinking of the parent-god's body in the forms of magically potentiating food and wine (as exemplified in the ancient worship of Melitta and Mithra).
2.  The temple hymns, sung and played in the simple, repetitive, hypnotic cadences of a mother's lullaby—and often resulting in "temple sleep." Such escapist trances could then be varied with food, drink, and sexual indulgences to be triply enjoyed, since they also honored one's permissive and accommodating gods.
3.  The "laying on of hands" and "anointing" to cure an injured bodily part—a direct reminiscence of the soothing parental stroking of an injured child, as still sought by the emotionally immature avid of masseurs, chiropractic, or "sensitivity experiences."
4.  The ethereal, elevating emphasis on the "spiritual"—a concept as fundamental to life as is the neonate's first breath or *spiritus,* following which he is variously *inspired,* acquires an *esprit de corps,* becomes *dispirited* or *desperate* and eventually *expires* so that his immutable *spirit* can begin life anew. Here, too, the physician-priest functions in knowing the Spiritual World and purveying professed contrition and remorse to the Spirits of our Fathers, who then require only a small tithe and penance with which to vacate the horrors of eternal punishment. Meanwhile, the temple then and now furnished a divinely protected sanctuary from earthly stresses and problems.

Finally, the priest also mediated the supreme promise of all religions—or, for that matter, of all "scientific" systems—the conquest, through power and life eternal, of man's most grim and implacable enemy, death itself.

## ANXIETIES IN THE JUDEO-CHRISTIAN TRADITION

Historically, the ancient Hebrews conceived of an eternal struggle within each man between the Spirit of Evil *Yetzer ha'Rah* and the Spirit of Good *Yetzer ha'Tov* (as epitomized also in the *Hindu Siva* vs. *Vishnu* or the Taoist *Yin* vs. *Yang*). St. Augustine authoritatively advised strict austerity and Ambrosian religious grace for everyone—but only after he himself had explored Manichaean permissiveness and had eventually tired of his youthful diversions. However, most men, when anxious, reverted to patterns of physical defense, group action, or magical maneuvers. Thus, when the Black Death terrorized Europe for three hundred years (and Michelangelo confessed "no thought is born in me that has not Death engraved on it"), Christian men first tried their futile fasts, fires, and philters; when these failed, Queen Elizabeth hanged anyone who dared approach Windsor Castle, Jews were slain by the tens of thousands to appease the gentle Christ, and George Wicher (1625) recorded the human paradox that:

> Some streets had churches full of people weeping.
> Some others Tavernes had, rude revelles keeping.

Pascal, despite his Jansenite mysticism, was still fearful:

> When I consider the brief span of my life, swallowed up in the eternity before and behind it, the small space that I fill, or even see, engulfed in the intimate immensity of spaces which I know not, and which know not me—I am afraid.

Only when the threats of plagues and religious wars abated could men resume the intellectualized self-assertions of Descartes' *"Cogito, ergo sum"* or Spinoza's gentler solipsism:

> I saw that all the things I feared, and which feared me had nothing good or bad in them save insofar as my mind is affected by them. . . . Fear cannot be without hope, nor hope without fear (for) all is Nature and God.

Subsequent emphathizers with man's dilemma compounded other existential prescriptions: Kafka pleaded piteously with man's unknown persecutors; Kant structured the world according to his solipsistic "categories," Schopenhauer imperiously subjugated the universe to his Will and Idea; Nietzsche extolled the amoral super-man; Goethe (emulating Luther) used his inkwell to defy the Devil himself, and Thoreau sought an escapist Walden. Monothetically, Marx advocated revolution leading to the abolition of politico-economic controls; Comte tried to reduce all sociology to a mathematical science, Santayana admired the "beauty" of other forms of theology, and Kierkegaard abandoned all reason in favor of an intensity of experience that was at once an acknowledgment and a defiance of a death-dealing God—an heroic stand that, minus even the comforts of faith, was also assumed variously by Sartre and the late Albert Camus. Yet man's ultimate (Ur-) anxieties ever remained and necessitated what we may call his characteristic ultimate (Ur-) fantasies and Ur-adaptations.

## The Evolution of Man's Ur-Defenses

To give this topic more specific psychologic as well as evolutionary depth, let us again put ourselves in the position of a paleolithic ancestor who, cursed above all other creatures with apprehensive imagery, saw every natural phenomenon as an ominous threat, every living creature, including those of his own kind, as a potential enemy, and every tomorrow as a measureless vista of uncertainty without predictable order or mercy. What could Stone Age man think and do to save his sanity—and what have his descendants thought and done ever since? For that matter, it could be pointed out that setting the stage forty millennia ago is unnecessary inasmuch as man's physical, social, and cosmic insecurities are, if anything, greater now than they were then. *Ergo,* throughout our history the adaptive faiths and maneuvers we developed in order to avert stark panic were these three:

*First, an Illusion of Physical Invulnerability and Possible*

*Immortality*. This was an immediate necessity, since injury, disease, and senescence not only impaired our necessary physical competence to control the material universe about us, but posed the unthinkable threat and terror of death. We countered these challenges by many devices: All of medicine is a quest for strength and longevity, and in our other sciences and technologies we seek to extend our power over the myriad forces that ever menace us— even though the robots we invent for this purpose so often turn into Frankensteins.

*Second, the Hope of Brotherly Love*. Since we live in an increasingly crowded and dangerous world, this very circumstance posed our next problem, namely, that *our neighbor could preempt that world instead of helping us in our need, or employ his weapons against us before we could turn ours on him*. The paradox of our current age still is that whereas each of us is required to call everyone else his friend, each really suspects that the other may be a rival or just possibly an enemy. Put in terms of cultural evolution, the long-sought "missing link between ape and man" has long since been discovered: *It is us*. Hence, social distrust must again be countered by a second wishful fantasy: The world really *is* full of allies put there to cherish and serve us. Insofar as this hope has been effective, men have indeed expanded their allegiances from the family through the clan, tribe, and nation to the hope of world brotherhood; insofar as it has failed, larger and larger alliances of men have also tried to exterminate each other—and may yet succeed.

*Third, a Quest for a Celestial Order*. All this made man's final anxiety all the more poignant: Even were he to master everything on earth and pool all his capacities in a well-regimented global society, would men even then be more than an ant colony crawling about on an insignificant pebble mocked by a vast and impenetrable cosmos hardly sensed by their puny antennae? "Perish the thought!" say we; on the contrary, our profound philosophies can explain the entire universe. Alternatively we are the Chosen People of the God (and how different each of our variously revealed portraits of Him) Who devised all Creation for our exclusive delectation; indeed, since He is also our Omnipotent Servant,[1] we can secure external bliss by the very techniques of appeal, bribery, or (as a last resort) obedience that once worked well on our mortal parents. This in no way affirms or denies the "truth" of any metaphysical or theologic system; as scientists, we merely explore their origins and examine their functions.

## QUASI-SCIENTIFIC ROOTS OF CURRENT THERAPIES

After the Reformation, a charismatic Cromwellian lieutenant named Valentine Greatrakes ("the Stroaker") was among the first to claim that he could "purge the bodie of evil humores" without clerical sanctions, merely by "skillfulle massage." Thousands of people flocked to his "clinic" to have this self-assured healer pat and soothe them as though they were children, just as, again, thousands of people today are certain they obtain relief from chiropractic, osteopathy, or acupuncture.

A century and a quarter after Greatrakes, there lived the unwitting founder of many other "modern" therapeutic techniques: Anton Mesmer, whose system was based on the belief that when he made certain movements with his head or hands he could influence others without touching them. By a spurious analogy common in the field of therapy, Mesmer called this effect *animal magnetism* and related it to the "astrologic attractions" of stars and planets. To communicate this, people would "contact" each other in intimate groups, fall into trances, dream, have highly emotional (including erotic) reactions, and awake claiming to feel not only cured but exhilarated and "inspired"; compare "training" (T-) and "sensitivity" groups today.

Mesmer's methods were, of course, highly intriguing, and literally entranced a great many influential people. In another

---

[1] Michelangelo's greatest theologic as well as artistic subtlety may be that his Sistine Chapel painting may be interpreted obversely as depicting Adam giving life to God.

curious parallel with the current training of psychoanalysts, anyone could apply to a Mesmeric Institute to be personally mesmerized; then, after a certain number of "controlled" mesmeric sessions, he could be certified as an accredited mesmerist and belong to official national and international Mesmeric Societies that published erudite Journals of Mesmerism. He could then treat people according to the Society rules, but if he sought new and better methods, there was a good deal of discussion about his "loyalty" and a reconsideration of his "professional qualifications." Mesmer was, however, quite sincere in his theories and, as was the case with Freud a century later, felt himself martyred by the medical men of the day. Indeed, he remained convinced that he had discovered a universal system of healing. So he had, in the sense that he had once again tapped a basic human yearning for a trusting, regressive relationship that had been practiced in the temples of Mesopotamia and Egypt and in the Asklepeidae of classical times. There, too, in a setting of diminished light, with a central altar for concentrated attention, priests had intoned their simple, repetitive, rhythmic chants known to all mothers or kindergarten teachers who calm their troubled children with the soothing repose of lullabies.

Although Mesmer was eventually discredited and died in poverty, his system resonated with so many human longings for individual healing, conjoint rapport, and mystic experience that from it there sprang many of our current cults, schools, and practices:

*The wearing of "magnetic belts,"* still advertised and sold throughout the "civilized" world. Hundreds of thousands of people buy these metallized girdles or diapers as a cure for disease and preventive of debility.

*Present-day hypnotism,* in which "hypnotists" of all degrees of naïveté perennially rediscover that many people like to depend upon and humor a person who wields supposedly esoteric powers, and forget that Bernheim once cautioned Freud: "It's a wise hypnotist that knows who's hypnotizing whom."

*The Christian Science Church,* founded with fanatic zeal and administrative genius by Mary Baker (later Eddy) after an American mesmerist named Phineas Quimby "cured" her of various hysterical disorders. With consummate effectiveness, this Church implicitly invokes all of the Ur-faiths as follows:

1.  A system of doctrinaire beliefs, propounded in its founder's book *Science and Health, with Key to the Scriptures,* which purportedly reveals not only all religious but all scientific truth.
2.  An almost universal kinship through more than three thousand Churches of Christ Scientists, so that no believer need ever feel alone anywhere in the Western world.
3.  A simple, repetitiously assertive set of "health directives," all the more effective for their obscure dogmatism.
4.  A church service that consists largely of readings from Mary Baker Eddy, endlessly reiterated, so that one feels familiar with all there is to know.
5.  Finally, the belief that a Christian Scientist is not confined to time or space; he can heal at any distance with divine power.

Predictably, a great many troubled, lonesome human beings join Christian Science churches or other organizations with similar beliefs and rituals and thereby find precious relief and comfort. No one can deny the tragedies that can result from the misapplication of such doctrines and practices, but no one can gainsay how much surcease is afforded to hundreds of thousands of troubled people avid of supposed physical, social, and religious verities— and as therapists, we can neither neglect nor deny anything that concerns and comforts humanity.

## Freud and Psychoanalysis

Freudian psychoanalysis is a more remote and complex derivative of Mesmerism that at first sight seems to differ from the others in assuming purely scientific import and content, and yet it, too, can best be understood in its historical perspectives.

Sigmund Freud (1856–1933) began by using various forms of hypnosis to command his patients to tell him what was troubling them in the form of a directed confessional. But since many patients resisted this, Freud abandoned hypnosis and instead directed his patients to say everything that occurred to them without conscious censorship or restraint, i.e., to use the technique of *free association*. They would then tell him, often with appropriate histrionics, about the recent stresses they thought—or wanted *him* to think—had caused their current difficulties. Freud called this *catharsis*, in the sense of ridding the mind of something noxious, and *abreaction* when the emotionality was intense and therefore seemed to relieve repressed tension. Concurrently, Freud's patients also found him to be interested and understanding rather than judgmental or punitive and thereby felt further relief in having found a confidant.

Freud postulated, however, that his patients must have been chronically troubled long before the relatively trivial happenings to which most of them attributed their recent difficulties; i.e., they must have been *sensitized by preceding experiences* that he directed his patients to recall. Predictably, most patients then began to "remember" (often falsely as in *screen memories*) supposed events in their adolescence and eventually their childhood that were then interpreted to the effect that previously *repressed* but inwardly disturbing threats, rejections, and disappointments had rendered the patient particularly sensitive to current insecurities, jealousies, fears, and conflicts. Thus for a time psychoanalysis consisted of covertly directed attempts to reconstruct childhood *traumas*, particularly the so-called *Oedipus complex* and other *libidinal conflicts*.

CASE 30 Free Associations on Primal Anxiety

"I remember that mother was supposed to have been very devoted and indulgent to me—and I suppose she was. I got everything I wanted, but then I got lots of things I didn't want too. I think she got father [a physician] to prescribe every rotten thing in his books for me, and she used to wheedle me till I took it. I took it and sometimes I puked on her, but I took it so she'd keep fussing. . . . Maybe I was scared too. Maybe she hated me. This I can't say I really remember, and maybe I'm just trying to act smart to please you or be my own analyst again, but I kind of remember a half-dream or maybe just a feeling I had even before I could talk—maybe at one or two. It was that I didn't want covers on me or a pacifier in my mouth, or maybe even the mattress at my back—I didn't know they were covers or pacifiers, but I couldn't *do* anything about it anyway and I was terrified. Later it seemed that I never really had any peace—like my mother and grandmother and everybody kept sticking things into my mouth or anus or flinging me around or diapering me any time they wanted to except that I really didn't know there were real people. . . . I could throw a tantrum and make such things stop, but they'd start again. . . . I don't know—maybe that's why I used to sneak downstairs and bang the big piano at night—my father said I used to do that when I was 3. I remember I liked it because the noise started and stopped when I did, even though my mother later made me use one finger and play a goddam tune. Maybe that's why I had to be top of my class at [a private boy's school], so nobody would help with my studies. Or maybe that's why I sleep separate from my wife now. I still can't stand anybody fussing with my body when I don't want them to—once when I was drunk I nearly strangled a woman at a party for slipping her hand inside my shirt. . . ."

Freud eventually began to recognize the importance of what almost every teacher, minister, physician, or other mentor had implicitly known: The therapist is inevitably regarded by the patient as a parental or other substitute or *surrogate* and is then treated as a protective mother, a punitive father, an erotic object, a rival or enemy, or in other roles *transferred* to the therapist from the patient's lifelong fantasies and interpersonal relationships. If then, by appropriate *transference interpretations,* the patient is led to recognize the artificial positions into which he forces not only the therapist but other people in his life, he may develop more realistic and effective patterns of behavior and thus resolve his personal and social difficulties. Freud thereby rediscovered and reformulated (sometimes unnecessarily fancifully and obscurely) various principles of human communication and clinical therapy that have been operative throughout the ages—and, of course, need still be applied if any form of treatment, including psychoanalysis, is to be successful.

## PSYCHOANALYSIS AS PERSONALITY THEORY

Concurrently, Freud evolved another aspect of psychoanalysis as a theory (*metapsychology*) of the development and vicissitudes of human behavior, replete with specialized terms and concepts. Since these have permeated much recent thought and writing, they require an additional review.

### THE STRUCTURE OF THE PERSONALITY[1]

The functions of the total personality were divided by Freud into three parts:

*The Id.* This is conceived to be a repository of the "instincts" or drives of the individual expressed as narcissistic, oral, anal, and genital libidinal tendencies, which constitute the *primary processes.* These are below the limen of the direct awareness of the individual, hence they comprise a large portion of what Freud reified as *the*

---

[1] With regard to Freud's self-admitted "metapsychologic mythology," it is interesting to note that in every age and developed culture from the Euphrates to the Arctic, man has projected three parameters of deified abstractions, supposedly representing his own triune nature. The first of these categories was composed of gods of blind, subterranean passion and fury, called variously Seth, Sin, Ahriman, Dionysus, Siva, Loki, or Beelzebub. To counteract these were demigods helpfully and rationally regulative of man's behavior on earth: Amon, Zoroaster, Apollo, Brahma, Thor, Quetzalcoatl, Jesus, Mohammed, and their beneficent kind. Above all these, however, towered awesome Beings who laid down harsh and incontrovertible edicts as to the conduct of the universe: Ra, Baal, Ahura Mazda, Zeus, Wotan, or Yahweh—They who must be obeyed because They can reward or punish without reason or appeal. And thus we have in man's most ancient imagery the prototypes of what Freud, in his correspondence with Albert Einstein, personified as the "neo-mythologic" Id, Ego and Superego, or the Eros and Thanatos of man's "psyche."

*Unconscious.* Opposed to the primal conations of the Id are the *repressive forces* of the *Ego,* which prevent inadmissible aggressive or erotic impulses from erupting into the awareness of the individual, pervading his conduct, and thus endangering his intrapersonal and social adjustments. In *dreams* this unconscious *censorship* and monitoring is relaxed, so that the undisciplined, unrealistic, unintegrated wishes of the Id, though still clothed in allegory and symbolism, appear in more easily recognizable forms. The atavistically sexual, aggressive, dependent, and narcissistic primary processes are likewise discernible, though less easily so, in fantasies, in free associations, in the inadvertencies of speech and action that constitute the *psychopathology of everyday life* and, of course, in neurotic and psychotic *symptom formation.*

*The Ego.* This designates a portion of the personality that adapts to "reality" by exercising a twofold function. On the one hand, the *conscious Ego* utilizes the information imparted by the senses, subjects these data to the discerning integrative processes of the intellect, and so evaluates the milieu in terms of available sources and means of gratification; concurrently, another portion of the Ego, largely unconscious, is "directed inward" to oppose the forces of the Id by the use of various specific *secondary processes* or *defense mechanisms.* In effect, the Ego is the interpretive, adaptive, and executive "part" of the personality, driven by the Id and conforming to the demands of the Superego.

THE MECHANISMS OF DEFENSE

In its attempts to find practicable compromises among the "imperious instinctual demands of the Id," the inhibitions and exhortations of the Superego, and the hard facts of external reality, the Ego uses various maneuvers ranging from "normal" through "neurotic" and "psychotic." These can be summarized as first described by Freud and later codified by his daughter Anna:

Suppression: the deliberate, willful exclusion of dangerous antisocial impulses, ideas, or emotions from awareness and action.

CASE 31 Conscious and Unconscious Factors in Suppression

An only son was subjected to a premature and tyrannical educational regimen by his father who, himself a frustrated and unsuccessful schoolteacher, wanted his child to become a "genius" and thus rescue the prestige of the family. The boy, though intelligent and mathematically gifted, rebelled against all learning but was pushed into advanced work by his relentless parent. By this time, the youth hated all teachers and their teachings and became almost unbearably sensitive to discipline by them. One day in a flash of resentment against a fancied slur in class (which he mistakenly thought was perceived by everyone) the boy felt a nearly overwhelming urge to strike his teacher and to stalk out of the classroom. However, he "reconsidered" the situation, suppressed his pride and anger and decided to stay; later, in fact, he apologized to the astonished instructor who had remained completely innocent throughout the patient's inner struggle. But the boy was never aware of how deeply the "sensible" decision he "deliberately" reached had really been influenced by many unconscious factors: the identification of every teacher, however kindly, with the tyrannical father; the equation of even mild aggression with unthinkable patricide; and the necessity he felt to placate the father–teacher by an apology for the impulse of sudden hostility he had experienced.

Repression: the internal, unconscious inhibition of unacceptable motivations or affects so that, although they remain operative, they are not directly sensed or expressed.

CASE 32 Anxiety Reaction with Repression

A young lady came to the psychiatrist from her physician bearing a sealed note that read: "There is something queer about Miss ——. She has a blood-pressure of 240/142, and has probably been severely hypertensive for at least two years, but she says she has had no symptoms at all. Next week she is to have a complete sympathectomy, and she knows it is a fairly dangerous operation with probably a long and uncomfortable convalescence. But that doesn't seem to faze her either. Is she schizophrenic?"

True enough, when the patient—a winsomely attractive girl—was interviewed, she stated at first that, apart from occasional slight headaches, she "felt fine," and if the doctors thought she needed a serious operation, "the thing to do was to have it and not worry about it." Far from schizoid, however, was her sympathetic interest in everything and everyone about her, her facile affective reactions to all topics under discussion other than her own illness, and the friendly rapport she rapidly cultivated with the interviewer. Briefly, her psychiatric history revealed that her parents were cultured, artistic people devoted to their only daughter, that her home life had been relatively happy, and that she had been popular and successful at school and college—far more because of her ingratiating good humor and extroverted activities than her outstanding scholastic abilities. Early in life she had become interested in dramatics, had cultivated her voice under expert tutelage, and had starred in high school and college productions. A talent scout had heard her performance in one of these and had offered a contract for a minor singing role in a traveling operetta company after her graduation. The patient had been overjoyed, since she considered this as a start on a long-coveted stage career. Correspondingly great, therefore, was her disappointment when a routine physical examination for participation in actors' equity insurance revealed a serious degree of vascular hypertension that made a stage career apparently impossible for her. The patient's reaction to her disappointment was characteristic: She denied the seriousness of her illness to herself as well as to others, trustingly put herself into the hands of her physicians, and blithely planned to fulfill her contract after the "slight delay" of her operation. The defensive nature of this behavior, however, became apparent when the patient later confided that she had really been suffering from headaches, tinnitus, vertigo, fatigue, and other symptoms for several years, had wished to seek help, but had feared to do so because a serious disorder might be diagnosed. Finally, she confessed, with what was now an unconvincing attempt at nonchalance, that if through some inconceivable chance she could not continue her dramatic career, she would hardly consider life really worth living and suicide would be the only solution.

Here, then, was an individual whose denial of symptoms

was a compulsive device designed to mitigate otherwise catastrophic anxiety. By this defense she had kept herself tolerably cheerful, active, and socially useful, unfortunately, at the expense of neglecting the premonitory signs of a dangerous illness. The unusual, yet significant, feature of the case was the persistence of this denial of anxiety up to the moment of the psychiatric interview.

COURSE

Under sympathetic encouragement the patient was able to confess almost to the full her doubts and trepidations during the course of several interviews. Some of these were characterized by marked emotional "catharsis," including tears and protestations of hopelessness and discouragement, yet each such affective discharge, since it evoked empathic acceptance and reassurances, left the patient quieter and more receptive to realistic orientations. Finally, when she changed her attitude from a brittle anxiety-ridden pretense of unconcern to a more confident and stable courage, a Smithwick sympathectomy was planned and performed. She cooperated well in preoperative and convalescent therapy and left the hospital with a relatively well-adjusted acceptance not only of her physical limitations but also of her remaining capacities for creative and relatively happy living.

Displacement: the transfer of meaning and value from one object, situation, or function to another; e.g., a girl may deviate postcoital concern over her "soiled genitals" into obsessive–compulsive oral hygiene.

CASE 33 Compulsive Displacement

A boy of sixteen, troubled by open conflicts with his fanatically religious father and currently much concerned by his "secret sin of masturbation," had developed a number of compulsive rituals that had become annoying to his family. Among these was a peculiar insistence on repeating grace, not once but three times, before every meal. The father, enraged by what appeared to be a travesty of the usual family custom, had begun to force the boy to eat without his preliminary prayers. The patient had attempted to comply but found himself unable to do so because of trembling, palpitation, "all-gone feeling in the stomach," sweating, and more particularly, a "lump in the throat" that made swallowing impossible. These symptoms abated only slowly if he was ordered from the table, but disappeared promptly if he were permitted to go through his ritual and then discard his first bite of food. Investigation indicated that the three prayers were intoned to expiate guilt not only for his masturbation but also for "bad thoughts about mother and father;" so also, he felt compelled to renounce his first mouthful of food before he "deserved to be given more." He was sorry that his family "had to suffer so for my sake—but they will go to heaven and they say I won't—so we'll be even." When permitted his rituals, he felt little anxiety; when they were proscribed, the symptoms described above inevitably recurred.

Substitution: the replacement of motives, concepts, or acts by others with a lesser charge (*cathexis*) of anxiety; e.g., devotion to pets in a mother deprived of child care.

## CASE 34 Reaction Formation and Substitution

The neglected, childless wife of a wealthy alcoholic could satisfy neither her marital nor maternal longings and, in compensatory overreaction, became openly antisocial and misanthropic. However, she professed a great love for animals, provided a home for strays, kept numerous dogs, cats, parrots, and canaries (which not infrequently maimed or killed each other) and organized militant antivivisection movements. Finally, she became so fanatic and irrational in the latter activity that defensive legal action and adverse publicity finally induced her family to persuade her to seek psychiatric help.

Reaction formation: the *substitution* of contrasting patterns for those repressed; e.g., heterosexual promiscuity (Don Juanism) in a latent homosexual.

## CASE 35 Antisocial Reaction Formation

An intelligent, attractive girl who had been brought up in

circumstances of frustrating sexual temptation by an irresponsible, negligent, and eventually parasitic father became a prostitute later in life with the following (relatively common) pattern: She displaced her filial ambivalence to a dependent, seemingly "masochistic," but actually preemptive and exploiting relationship with an underworld procurer, and expressed her hostility to all other men in her complete indifference to how many others she frustrated, robbed, infected, or blackmailed.

Sublimation: the channelization of repressed impulses into socially approved conduct; e.g., voyeurism into artistic photography.

## Case 36 Sublimation and Rationalization

Many professional workers like to think—and some of them insist—that they became nurses, doctors, ministers, social workers, etc., because of an altruistic ache to help suffering humanity, although a few admit that desires for economic security and social prestige played some role. However, on franker and deeper introspection, and certainly under objective analysis, both levels of motivation can usually be traced to comparatively primitive needs: "security" resolves itself into adequate food, warmth, and shelter; "social prestige" protects, implements, and enhances these basic satisfactions plus, of course, providing better opportunities for mating and procreation.

Denial: the refusal to accept unwelcome reality; e.g., internally, one's true motivations, or externally the news of the death of a loved person or the success of a hated one.

## Case 37 Hysterical Amaurosis with Homosexuality

A twenty-four-year-old girl was brought for therapy with the statement that she "had been blinded by a sudden flash of light" two days previously. Careful examinations revealed no abnormalities of the eyes or nervous system, yet the patient insisted that she could barely distinguish light from darkness. In fact, she stumbled painfully over furniture when permitted to walk unguarded and was seen to do so even when she thought herself unobserved. The history revealed that for the preceding six years the patient had been the active homosexual partner of an older woman with whom she lived. During the past year she had become intensely jealous of another girl who, she thought, was replacing her in her roommate's affections. Two days before her admission she had followed her roommate to this girl's house and had seen them enter her rival's car in a darkened garage. When the two women began to drive away, she had stumbled into the path of the automobile, had been "blinded by the lights," knocked over, and had narrowly escaped being seriously injured. When picked up off the street, she stated that her vision was gone, ad she had to be helped back to their home by her frightened and thoroughly contrite roommate. Characteristically, the patient professed little concern over her serious disability and was loath to enter the hospital. Hypnosis after preparatory therapy and a reconciliation with her roommate readily restored her sight, but the patient continued to regard her recovery as a miraculous "cure" of what she preferred to consider a purely organic ocular injury. Obviously, insight into the reality-denying and symbolically self-castrative nature of her hysterical blindness (in her dreams and fantasies her eyes seem symbolically equated with testicles) was too disturbing to be admitted to consciousness.

Undoing: symbolic reversal of a guilt-inducing event; e.g., erecting eternal monuments to persecuted martyrs.

### CASE 38 Psychophysiologic Undoing by Identification

A fifty-four-year-old spinster complained that the right side of her face and neck was affected by severe pains, the cause of which could not be determined by physical and laboratory examinations, and that persisted despite all medication. The psychiatric history revealed that the patient, a shy, isolated person, had but one friend—a neighbor whose husband some six months previously had developed a malignant right cervical tumor. On the patient's recommendation he had been taken to the university hospital, where he died in a few weeks. The patient's friend, in her depth of grief, had turned furiously on the patient with the accusations that the latter had "sent him to die" and that, had she not done so, he would still be alive. Soon after this the patient herself developed facial pains very like those of the deceased husband and promptly entered the university hospital with the emphatic statement that she herself was certain it was "the best hospital in the country." Other data, as expected, revealed another and less conscious dynamism than this relatively simple one of self-justification: The attachment of the two women friends had bordered on homosexuality, and the patient was symbolically replacing the dead husband.

Therapy consisted of simple reassurances to the patient that "nervous pains" in any part of the body could be caused by "worry and aggravation," and concurrent reexplanations to the widow that her husband's illness had been inevitably fatal despite the best of treatment. Once a reconciliation between the women had been effected, the patient's pains responded promptly to placebos and mild massage, and she was discharged symptom-free.

Phobia formation: dread of an object, situation, or act unconsciously symbolic of threat or conflict; e.g., fear of heights (*acrophobia*) in a patient who equates this with dangerously "phallic" erection or eminence.

## CASE 39 Erotogenic Phobias

An unhappily married woman developed a fear of being alone in the street or in "high places." Analysis of her previously unconscious motivations and fantasies showed that such fears arose because of repressed temptations to erotic exhibitionism and promiscuity; significantly, she experienced much less anxiety in either situation when she was accompanied by a member of her own family, since under such conditions her self-control was supplemented and reinforced, and her feelings of regressive dependence were strengthend.

Obsessive–compulsive reactions: consciously presented thoughts and/or acts that deny, conceal, or *undo* repressed impulses; e.g., Lady Macbeth's incessant preoccupation with washing her hands to dispel the traces of homicide.

CASE 40 "Ablutomania"

A thirty-year-old woman developed such severe washing rituals that she was compelled to spend practically her entire day scrubbing her hands, the dishes, the rugs, the basement steps, the toilet bowl, and almost every other object about the house. Her history revealed an insecure childhood spent in poverty and squalor, to which she had reacted with ambivalence toward her ignorant, foreign-born parents and a defensive overemphasis on "culture and cleanliness." She contracted a loveless marriage at eighteen mainly "to get myself a decent home" and for more than a decade her husband, an insensitive, easy-going individual, tolerated her sexual frigidity and her frequently annoying overmeticulousness in running their home and in disciplining their only son. A year before her hospital admission, however, two circumstances seriously disturbed her precarious marital adjustments: Her husband secured a job as foreman in a steel plant and moved their home to the noisy, smoky vicinity of the factory, and her son began to emancipate himself from her preemptive discipline and to cultivate extra-familial contacts in the new neighborhood. The patient almost immediately wished to move back to their former isolated home in the suburbs and rationalized her desires by stating that "no one could live in all this smoke and dirt." The husband and son, however, both refused to surrender their respective advantages in the new environment, whereupon the patient began a series of washing compulsions that became more elaborate and prolonged until she had time for little else. When analyzed, these rituals were seen to subserve at least two purposes: They were at the same time a counter-phobic denial of, and a symbolic return to, the dreaded, yet safe, squalor of her childhood, and they also served as concealed avenues of "anal–erotic" aggression against her faithless son and husband, whose lives were made miserable but without possibility of recourse against the patient's pathetic illness. Needless to say, the patient could not recognize either of these motivations; all she knew, before therapy slowly established partial insight and better adaptations, was that she "had to keep washing" or else suffer inexplicable but scarcely bearable fears that somehow her husband, her child, or she herself "might get sick and die if I left a speck of dirt —and it would be all my fault."

Psychosomatic symptom formation: expression in musculo-skeletal or internal visceral (*organ neurotic*) dysfunctions of repressed attitudes and conflicts; e.g., chronic joint pains and high blood pressure in a patient who lives in a state of repressed but continued anxiety or rage.

CASE 41 Psychophysiologic Pseudocyesis with Amenorrhea and Vomiting

A twenty-one-year-old girl was referred from a physician with a note that, whereas he had been unable to detect any signs of pregnancy, the patient not only insisted that she was pregnant, but also attributed her anorexia, vomiting, amenorrhea, abdominal pains, and general irritability to this condition. Physical examination showed only a gaunt, markedly undernourished girl who affected a posture and mode of abdominal relaxation that gave her the appearance of early pregnancy. There were, however, no other physical signs of this, and, as previously, the Aschheim–Zondek and *Rana pipiens* tests were negative.

The history and mental status examinations revealed a wealth of neurotic and borderline psychotic patterns that need not be detailed here. One was of particular psychosomatic interest:

The patient's father, an irresponsible, alcoholic psychopath, had seduced the girl into sex play at an early age and had begun to attempt intercourse with her when she was about twelve. This failed primarily because the patient's genitalia remained infantile, but the two continued the practice of mutual masturbation. At eighteen the patient, jealous of a younger sister whom the father had begun to prefer, eloped to another city with a young man who, after a single frustrating sexual relationship with her, "did the right thing" and married her. The patient, however, was unhappy in her new home; intercourse with her husband again proved impossible, and after a few months he lost patience and brought her back to her parents. There the patient discovered that her sister was illegitimately pregnant and immediately suspected her father —a suspicion soon confirmed by the sister. The patient missed her next menstrual period, began to believe herself pregnant by her own husband, and thereafter rapidly developed the pseudocyetic abdominal enlargement, vomiting, dietary idiosyncrasies, and emotional instability that brought her to the clinics.

COURSE

Under Amytal narcosis administered as part of the initial sedation for her insomnia and her restlessness, the patient furnished additional material that indicated that her unconscious desires to be pregnant were compounded by a jealous identification with the sister, together with aggressively tinged wishes to reveal her own incestuous relationships with the father; a longing to force her way back into the family circle as a prospective mother forsaken and requiring prenatal care; a similar wish to regain her husband in a protective, nonsexual relationship; or finally, failing all these, a regressive preemptive flight to the haven of a maternity hospital.

The patient showed initial improvement under routine care and was fairly easily induced to relinquish her fantasies of being pregnant. However, she became increasingly demanding of special foods, individual visiting hours and other indulgences; developed uncompromising animosities to student nurses and other sister surrogates on quite fanciful pretexts; and finally became exceedingly uncooperative. Later, distortions of affect and ideation became apparent; for instance, the patient, with a peculiarly remote equanimity, stated that an elderly ward janitor had been hypnotizing her. Commitment was therefore recommended, but the family refused and took her home. There she ate very little, began vomiting frequently, and finally became so cachectic that the possibility of Simmonds' disease was seriously considered. She died in a sanatorium a short time later.

Conversion reactions: focalized sensorimotor (*hysterical*) dysfunctions; e.g., the onset of anesthesia and paralysis of the right arm in a man nearly overcome by an impulse to kill his father. (See Case 27.)

Distortions of affect: the emotional excesses of *euphoria* or *melancholy* (as in *manic–depressive states*) or the blunting or inappropriateness of affective reactions (as in *schizo-phrenia*).

## Case 42 Hypomania

A wealthy executive, forty-eight years of age, was brought to the hospital by a business associate who stated that the patient "had been running himself so ragged with too much work and too much play" that his friends had insisted that he come to the hospital for a "check-up and a rest-cure." Further questioning revealed that for the preceding four months the patient had been working intensely but erratically, making quick business decisions that sometimes produced brilliant results, but as often proved unsound and unprofitable. Moreover, his social behavior had become impulsive and unpredictable; for instance, he had twice abruptly adjourned business conferences in the midst of serious work with a sudden invitation to everyone present "to quit, have a drink, and come play golf at my club." On the first occasion a few present had good-naturedly accepted, but while he was driving them to the golf course the patient suddenly expanded his invitation to include a complete week-end for everyone at his country home two hundred miles away, and had been only with difficulty dissuaded from heading there immediately. In his executive capacities he continued with similar impetuosity to arrange unnecessary trips and conferences and to propose extravagant promotional schemes; similarly, in his entertainments for the firm's customers, his restlessness, unnecessary lavishness, excessive drinking, and forced gaiety had been increasingly embarrassing to his friends. These insisted, however, that the patient had previously been a sober, stable, and rather undemonstrative individual.

In the hospital the patient's behavior was characteristically pseudomanic. He dressed in flashy pajamas and loud bathrobes and was otherwise immodest and careless about his personal appearance. He neglected his meals and rest hours and was highly irregular, impulsive, and distractable in his adaptations to ward routine. Without apparent intent to be annoying or disturbing he sang, whistled, told pointless off-color stories, visited indiscriminately, and flirted crudely with the nurses and female patients. Superficially, he appeared to be in high spirits; yet one day when he was being gently chided over some particularly irresponsible act, he suddenly slumped in a chair, covered his face with his hands, began sobbing, and cried, "For God's sake, doc, let me be. Can't you see that I've just got to act happy?" This reversal of mood was transient, and his seeming buoyancy returned in a few moments; nevertheless, during a Sodium Amytal interview his defensive euphoria again dropped away, and he burst into frank sobbing as he clung to the physician's arm. He then confided that during the preceding year he had begun to suspect, with some reason, that his young second wife whom he "loved to distraction" had tired of their marriage and had been unfaithful to him. He had accused her of this, and she had replied, almost indifferently, with an offer of divorce. His pride had been greatly wounded, but to salvage it, avoid the scandal of a second divorce and to keep her as long as possible, they had agreed that she take an extended European tour and postpone her decision until her return. During her absence he had been obsessively torn by suspense, jealousy, and anger; could no longer take an interest in his work; and had lost sleep, strength and weight. He consulted his family physician for the latter symptoms, but the doctor, after finding little physically wrong with him, had simply advised him "to forget your business troubles [sic], play a bit more golf, get about more and enjoy yourself." He had followed this advice with compulsive intensity, but with the abreactive exaggeration that had eventually led to his admission to the hospital.

Needless to say, this account by the patient as to the reasons for his disturbances of mood and behavior was far from complete, but served to initiate further confidences in later interviews. Thus, the patient confessed that during the past several years he had begun to feel that his place near the head of a business concern was being threatened by younger, more energetic, and better-trained men, in competition with whom he himself had thought it necessary to become ultra-"progressive" in his executive tasks. In private life, too, he had become afraid of being considered "just a nice old has-been" and had therefore begun to indulge in drinking, athletics, and exhibitionistic stag-party venery he didn't really enjoy. But perhaps his greatest defense against his obsessive fears of obsolescence has been his second marriage to a young, pretty, and popular girl whom he had, by offering her a life of wealth and ease, won away from more youthful admirers. The patient unconsciously prized his wife as a symbol of his own renewed youth; unfortunately, in his anxiety to prove his sexual competence, he had frequently been impotent with her and had then made their marriage almost intolerable by his reactive rages and jealousies. As a result she had very probably become unfaithful and was currently spending more of his money in Europe in anticipation of an eventual divorce.

Under a regimen of rest, sedation, physiotherapy, and a gradual working-through of his emotional difficulties preparatory to extramural readjustments in his business, social, and marital affairs, the patient's hypomanic tension abated; and he regained relative equanimity with attendant improvement in behavior.

Fantasy formation: a recourse to wishful thought and imagery that may range from normal *day-dreams* to the irrational convictions (*delusions*), sensory misinterpretations (*illusions*), and vivid imaginations (*hallucinations*) of the *psychotic*.

CASE 43 Gross Stress Reaction with Acute Neurotic and Psychotic Symptomatology—"Reality" Therapy

An American veteran of the North African campaign in World War II recounted the following experience: On a solitary reconnaissance mission deep into the desert he had taken prisoner and disarmed a wounded German, but on attempting to find their way back to the Allied lines both men became lost among the rapidly shifting outposts of the opposing armies. The American, knowing that their supply of food and water was minimal, had put the German and himself on strictly equal rations of their joint resources. By the evening of the second day their canteens were almost empty, and both faced the prospect of perishing in the desert. This "reality threat," of course, caused intense anxiety, but the point at issue is that even under such starkly simple circumstances the American's notions of "reality," as he later "realized," were largely of his own imagining. Actually, he could easily have either abandoned or killed his prisoner and thus more than doubled the chances of his own survival. Indeed, no one need have been the wiser, and many, had they known of the act, would have approved it as a proper retribution for the many Nazi atrocities reputedly being committed at the time. Instead, the American, who had been raised in a Quaker tradition of mercy and " self-sacrifice," reacted in a quite different way. He admitted that impulses to rid himself of his prisoner kept recurring, but to guard against them he kept his automatic unloaded and his knife deeply buried in his pack. In overcompensation, he was outwardly exceedingly solicitous about the welfare of his charge, who by this time was nearly blind and almost completely helpless. His own anxiety, nevertheless, continued to increase, especially when, on the third night, he began having vivid dreams that his prisoner was attacking him and must instantly be disposed of. On the fourth day a mild delirium set in, with the peculiarly poignant content that if he gave the German the rest of their water and himself committed suicide, he would be rewarded for an act foreordained by God by being immediately translated into Heaven to join his adored mother. During this time, too, many other significant "neurotic" and semipsychotic reactions occurred: transient but intense rages directed at his empty canteen bottle (sometimes conceived of as a dried and flattened breast); abortive masturbation; numerous mirages of verdant oases; regressive visions of his childhood home in Pennsylvania, of peaceful landscapes that somehow resolved themselves into the kindly countenance of a long-forgotten Quaker schoolmistress; direct hallucinations of his father's voice, which he answered aloud in childish repartee; and other such patterns of manifest symbolic significance. Fortunately, all of them were cut short by the appearance of a reconnoitering British tank that happened on the scene and rescued them both. At its mere appearance, *and even before he had been supplied with water, food, and shelter,* his panic and pseudodelirium vanished in a rush of joy and relief.

CASE 44  Schizophrenic Hallucinations

A twenty-three-year-old woman with a markedly schizoid

personality, paranoid tendencies, and precarious "reality" adjustments was informed by her husband that he was soon to be drafted into the army. She reacted with feelings of deep insecurity and fantasies of regression to former sexual, familial, and other relationships. Two days later she asked him if it was not possible that his selection had been "arranged" by a girlhood paramour of hers who had "fixed" it so that he could in this manner have the patient for himself. The husband, busy with his army induction, dismissed this as just a bit more bizarre than her "usual queer ideas," and departed on schedule. Soon, however, the patient began to detect a peculiar taste in her food and noted that she was continually aroused sexually; this confirmed her suspicions that her paramour was drugging her food so as to seduce her. One morning a week later, after an erotic dream, she awoke to "see" this man "leering" into her window and concluded that he had also hypnotized her while she slept. She upbraided him and he disappeared, only to return that afternoon. This time she called the police, who found no evidence of an intruder; however, at her demand, they issued a warrant for his arrest. Fortunately, it was found that the accused had moved to another city several weeks before his alleged attempts at poisoning and seduction. The Red Cross was called in, communicated with the husband at his army camp, arranged for a psychiatric examination of the woman, and supervised her commitment to a private sanatorium.

Regression: the resumption, under stress, of modes of behavior that had been more satisfactory in earlier periods of life; e.g., the recurrence of infantile postures in *catatonia* or childlike conduct in *hebephrenia.*

## CASE 45 Acute Regression—Combat Neurosis

A soldier, normally well-disciplined and self-reliant but subjected overlong to physical exhaustion and the unremitting hell of combat and carnage in the ever-present shadow of death, eventually reached his limit of tolerance and thereafter showed a gradual dissolution of adult habit patterns and an accelerating return to childlike and then infantile behavior. First, his intellectual interests and activities became dulled and his affective reactions progressively more labile and primitive; concurrently, he began to neglect habits of personal hygiene, even to the point of careless evacuation and soiling. Next he became preoccupied with hazy dreaming of the comforts and security of his own home; finally, in sudden desperate denial of all mature considerations of prestige, duty, discipline, or even physical danger, he abandoned his weapons, cried out against all about him, and fell to the earth sobbing piteously and inconsolably for his mother. During this extreme reaction, threats of further discipline or even death were useless; the soldier had to be evacuated as a psychiatric casualty, permitted for the time being to cling emotionally to a kind therapist as a parent-surrogate, and thereafter treated by every means at hand to restore his self-confidence, his group loyalties and his normal defenses against anxiety lest his regression become fixed at the level of phobic, helpless passivity.

In military psychiatry, reactions such as these are relatively frequent, and their accompanying regression may take a rapid course from premonitory to acute stages; fortunately, however, prompt and skillful treatment may reverse the process. In civilian neuroses (except those occurring after catastrophes) regressive behavior is less extreme but more chronic and more subtly intertwined with other neurotic defenses. Moreover, the secondary regressive gains of the neuroses (such as relief from onerous responsibilities, repression or deviation of aggression, and the attainment of protective familial or other care) are less easily controlled than in military practice, and therefore make the treatment of chronic civilian neuroses usually more complex and difficult.

A military trainee without adequate preparation or "seasoning" is suddenly subjected to the destruction and immediate personal danger attendant on front-line combat. All his motivations are, of course, self-preservative, but he cannot implement them through immediate escape because, at the same time, deeply ingrained and contrary patterns of self-preservation through patriotism, group loyalties, hostility against a common enemy and considerations of his social safety confine him to the battlefield. He is, therefore, torn among insistent but apparently mutually exclusive patterns of adaptation that make it impossible for him to resolve the situation by the usual devices of compromise, flight, or fight.

If, then, his integrative capacities are further weakened by fatigue, he becomes incapable of handling the disruptive internal stresses so engendered and begins to suffer overwhelming anxiety accompanied by severe physiologic dysfunctions, motor disturbances, alterations of consciousness, etc. At this point, he may actually welcome even a moderately serious wound or inflict one on himself and feel euphoria instead of pain while being evacuated. Thereafter, any threatened return to the site of his traumatic experiences, actual or fancied, induces a recurrence of his anxiety to the point of panic, and even in the relative safety of the base hospital he shows hypersensitivity and phobic reactions to any perceptual configurations symbolic of these experiences. For instance, bed-sides cannot be tolerated because they are reminiscent of the inescapable confinement of the foxhole. The buzz of a fly or the striking of a match produces reactions comparable to those produced by the dive of a strafing plane or the explosion of a mortar-shell (see works by Ross, Gillespie, Grinker, and Glass).

Projections and delusions: the attribution of one's own motivations, ideas, and actions to others, as in feelings of being hated and persecuted (*paranoia*) in a person who wishes to justify his hostile intent toward others.

CASE 46 Schizophrenic Distortions of Thought and Affect

Wanda ———, the daughter of intelligent and cultured Czech immigrants, came to this country at the age of eight and was raised in a marginal slum district, where her father, though an excellent artisan, eked out a poor living in his metal-working shop. Her older brother, a handsome, energetic lad, was the parents' favorite and received whatever indulgences the family could afford: E.g., he was supported through high school and into college, while the patient had to work to contribute to her own and her family's support. Wanda, too, was sent to a parochial and later a public high school where, by dint of her facile intelligence and application, she made excellent grades during the first two years. However, since her extracurricular time was so completely occupied and also because her early training had made her shy, hesitant, and self-effacing, she cultivated few social activities and no friends. Instead, her only interest lay in the secret writing of highly dramatic novelettes and plays. The favorite heroine in these productions was a poor but talented and beautiful girl who, despite various buffetings of fate, finally won fortune and acclaim for some artistic masterpiece. In an ambivalent reaction to her family, she became increasingly ashamed of her "un-Americanized" parents and her poor home surroundings; conversely, she professed great pride in her popular and successful brother, especially when, in 1941, he became a volunteer air force cadet. But this pride, too, was a private affair. After his departure from home, she became all the more reserved and solitary and, when otherwise unoccupied, began to indulge in long and fanciful daydreams, usually as to how she would become a nurse, join her brother in the American military forces, liberate Czechoslovakia from Russia, and herself become a world-renowned heroine. The parents were not unobservant of her progressive isolation and social desuetude and finally insisted that she stop working after school in order to have time for normal recreations and social contacts. The patient compromised by devoting her free time to Czech liberation activities but again selected solitary tasks, such as folding and addressing circulars at home. Other peculiarities of behavior appeared that indicated a developing delusional context: The patient suddenly decided to change her Slavic name to the Anglo-Saxon "W———" and thereafter became infuriated if anyone used her original name. The patient went out on a few dates on her parents' insistence but compared her companions openly and unfavorably to her idealized brother, violently resented their tentative sexual advances, and soon dropped further contacts in this directiion. Her grades during the last year of high school dropped rapidly, as her work became disorganized and fragmentary. Although a few of her teachers noted the patient's growing peculiarities, she was lost in the mass-education "platoon system" of the school and given no individual attention or guidance.

The break that precipitated her frank psychosis occurred under these circumstances: One day the family received word that the patient's brother, far from being a success in the air force, had actually been responsible for a serious accident and had been dismissed from training because of recklessness and incompetence. The patient's reaction to this news was definitely abnormal, she assured her parents that although the notice received was "possibly a joke," it was more probably the government's test of their loyalty and patriotism. Two days later the patient suddenly announced during a recital in class that her brother was now a leading ace of the war, and supported this assertion by displaying a newspaper bearing a photograph and description of a flyer who in no way resembled her brother. When these discrepancies were pointed out to her by an astonished teacher, she explained them in a mysterious, disconnected manner on the basis of "military secrecy" and asserted further—but with little emotion—that Russian spies who were in conflict with "American pilgrims" were after her at that moment not only because of her brother, but to prevent her "from writing a book that would give away my information to make Czechoslovakia greater than Russia." Since the patient's behavior was now obviously psychotic, she was hospitalized soon after this episode. By this time her ideation and speech, disjointed or frequently blocked at best, was rendered even more incoherent by occasional *neologisms*, such as "frisgrace," by which the patient apparently meant a combination of "fame" and "disgrace." She wrote long letters to her brother in the "Czechoslovak Air Force," but the manuscripts consisted of criss-cross undecipherable writing and were illustrated by unexplained symbolisms of intertwined forms. One other episode was significant: With great difficulty, the patient was one day induced to join a group in a simple game of throwing darts at little wooden dwarf-like figures. She played mechanically and desultorily until quite by accident she hit one of the male figurines, whereupon she suddenly recoiled, gestured wildly, and then fell to the floor in seeming oblivion. Later she explained vaguely that by her act she had not only "knocked her brother from the skies" but had, in some universal manner, injured all fliers everywhere.

An analysis of these and other fantasies and reactions indicated that this patient's delusional system, bizarre and unorganized as it was, nevertheless had specific meanings and subserved definitely compensatory functions. Thus, she displaced her reactive hostility toward parents onto a condemnation of their "foreign customs" and even their surname, yet indicated her aggressive yearnings for reunion with them by her allegiance to Czechoslovakia, her identifications with their favored son, and her rejections of social or sexual emancipations from the home. The brother-symbol at the same time served other purposes: It supported her claims to security in this country (reflected also in her fanatic patriotism, her alliance with "American pilgrims," etc.); it signified her own displaced masculine wishes; and it expressed her over-compensatory desires to rise from rejection and obscurity to fame and power through a delusional idealization of her brother. Nevertheless, her jealousies could not be denied, and they shone through in her literally self-paralyzing guilt when she hit the wooden figure with her dart and so "knocked him from the skies." However displaced and condensed these fantasies were, they still approached too closely to her deepest anxieties and therefore had to be robbed, in typical schizophrenic fashion, of continuity, organization, and emotional tone, especially when they dealt with symbolically pressing events.

*The Superego.* This denotes a "psychic apparatus" that directs the primal strivings of the Id, as modified by the Ego, into behavior that further conforms to the double standards of the conscience and of the Ego-Ideal.

THE CONSCIENCE

In this capacity the Superego is the repository of internalized prohibitions derived from the conflictful and traumatizing experiences of childhood, and thereby consists of multiple pervasive "don'ts" that can be paraphrased variously as "thou shalt not (orally) preempt and incorporate aggressively"; "thou shalt not (anally) soil and attack"; "thou shalt not (phallically) desire incest," and so on. In the early training of the child, these prohibitions derive cogency from two main sources: fear of physical punishment from parents or parent-surrogates or, far more serious to the helpless child, dread of loss of security should such parent-figures be displeased or injured by his actions. In this way, abnegation of dangerous and forbidden modes of behavior comes to be regarded as self-preservative and of ultimate *hedonic gain,* and thereby remains fixed in the adaptive patterns of the child. These self-

imposed *inhibitions,* if later threatened by temptation or transgressed even in fantasy, evoke *anxiety* or, if flouted in action,
occasion conscious apprehensions of varying intensity. Thus, the
*conscience* derives its regulative powers from unconscious but
persistent fears of punishment or deprivation—the ultimate source
of all *guilt.* Classic analytic theory holds that by the age of from
four to six years the child has already run the gamut of narcissistic,
incorporative, aggressive, and erotic urges and their limens of
retributions, hence his conscience is patterned relatively early in
life, and subsequent modifications become progressively more
difficult.[1]

THE "EGO-IDEAL"

This function of the Superego parallels and supplements the
conscience, but controls behavior less by fear of consequences than
by directing it toward cultural goals. As we have seen, during the
course of his social development the child derives such standards
from various persons important in his environment whom he thereafter strives to emulate; motivational analysis generally shows that
the child does this not for idealistic reasons but in a wishful attempt
to attain the fancied advantages and prerogatives of the exemplar
with whom he tries to identify. For instance, a little girl playing with
dolls is, in her own fancy, herself a "mother" with all her perquisites
and privileges; just as in later life she will dress and gesture like the
class belle or a popular actress so that she, too, can be a claimant
to adoration and influence. Similarly, male youngsters cherish the

---

[1]Margaret Mead has reported that in some cultures (as among the Arapesh),
late weaning and the encouragement of almost every form of oral satisfaction in children may establish feelings of infantile security that persist
into adult life and so contribute to the formation of a stable, content, and
relatively noncompetitive society. However, Gesell's dictum is here pertinent:
"It is very apparent that the human infant assimilates the cultural milieu
only by gradual degrees; that he has vast immunities to acculturation; that
his nervous system sets metes and bounds to what the societal group would
do for him; indeed, determines what is done. The culture is adapted to him,
primarily; he adapts when he is ready." Our present youth do not seem to
be quite as "ready to adapt."

trappings of glorified adulthood, from cowboy to astronaut, complete with hobbyhorses to space ships through which they can, in fancy, equate themselves with their powerful, feared, and envied elders. More specific identifications with the traits of parents, teachers, or group leaders, or, later, artists, conquerors or, for that matter, rebels or criminals, may permanently mold the Ego-ideal and so channel behavior into social or antisocial, successful or unsuccessful and thereby "normal" or "neurotic" channels.[1]

### ERIC ERIKSON'S DEVELOPMENTAL CONCEPTS

Erikson, a nonmedical psychoanalyst, discerns a succession of eight "epigenetic" conflicts, each leading to a corresponding affect or drive as follows:

> *Oral trust versus mistrust* (in early childhood), generating *hope*.
> *Autonomy versus shame* (in later childhood), generating *will*.
> *Genital initiative versus guilt* (in puberty), generating *purpose*.
> *Industry versus inferiority* (in education), generating *competence*.
> *Identity versus diffusion* (in youth), generating *fidelity*.
> *Adult intimacy versus isolation* (sexual and other), generating *love*.
> *Generality versus stagnation* (in middle years), generating *care*.
> *Ego integrity versus despair* (in later life), generating *wisdom*.

Erikson's clinical dynamics can be epitomized by dicta such as "the obsessive–compulsive has . . . too weak a will to be flexible"; the psychotic "mistrusts"; and the schizophrenic has an intractable "identity crisis." Erikson's appraisals of history can also be gathered

---

[1] The very word "mores" is the plural of the Latin *mos*, meaning social custom devoid of implications of normality or morality. Peters puts it trenchantly: "There is perhaps not a single vice in the code of our own society that some other group has not considered a virtue—murder, theft, dishonesty, torture, suicide, adultery and the rest." See also Westermarck, and Sumner and Keller (references in Masserman, 1955).

from his comment, "Only by an historical coincidence did he [Adolf Hitler] become representative of the negative identity of Germany. . . . Everything that the world had always criticized as German the Nazis made to appear positive and (*sic*—italics mine) *pretended* that it was what they really wanted." Relevant to the "battle of the sexes," Erikson urges men to "stop . . . considering peacefulness unmanly" so that women could "become more masculine" in running the world. As to therapy, Erikson states, "There is an historical continuity in the Judeo-Christian mind between soul-searching prayer and self-analysis"; ergo, psychoanalysis is "the treatment situation in which intellectual insight is *forced* to become emotional insight."

Erikson's writings are variously regarded, depending on whether such pronouncements are considered cryptic and insubstantial or oracular and illuminating.

Other modifications of psychoanalytic theory will be considered in the corresponding sections on therapy.

# Modern Modes of Therapy in Disorders of Behavior

## Pharmacologic

There are no specific medications for personality disorders, and all drugs are dangerous in overdose or prolonged intake. The following, however, when prescribed at proper times and in controlled amounts by a physician, may be temporarily useful.

SEDATIVES AND HYPNOTICS

Barbiturates, bromides, chloral hydrate, and paraldehyde calm agitation and induce sleep, but are habit-forming and toxic in excessive amounts. Because of rapid addiction, methadone and other opiates should never be used except under controlled medical supervision. Amphetamine compounds, such as Dexedrine, temporarily increase alertness, but may cause restlessness and circulatory, digestive, and sensory dysfunctions. In recent years, various so-called "antidepressant" and "analeptic" drugs (Nardil, Ritalin), have been advocated, but apart from tricyclics (Tofranil) much of their effect may derive from a wishful belief of physician and patient in their efficacy. Under the rubric of "tranquilizers," the milder meprobamates (Miltown, Equanil) are widely used, but their pharmacologic benefit is dubious, and they may also be addictive to the point of serious withdrawal symptoms. Of the other "ataractics," only the phenothiazines have been demonstrably effective, and then only when properly prescribed for schizophrenic disorders. Lithium salts have recently been advocated for manic–depressive cycles, but must be carefully regulated.

### Anti-epileptics

Dilantin, phenurone, and the barbiturates diminish the frequency of seizures and thus provide a margin of physical and psychologic relief, if their adverse effects on the liver, blood, and nervous system are properly controlled.

### Hormones

Thyroid may be prescribed in cretinoid mental deficiency, growth hormones in pituitary dwarfism, adrenocortical substances in debilitative states associated with adrenal disease and, as noted, ovarian extracts for symptomatic therapy during menopause. Other than this, and despite popular impressions to the contrary, hormones are either useless or dangerous in the therapy of personality disorders except when administered by a specialist for specific medical reasons.

### Vitamins

Metabolic deficiencies such as rickets (inadequacies in calcium or vitamin D intake), beriberi (thiamine and other B-complex substances), pellagra (nicotinic acid), nutritional anemia ($B_{12}$), or scurvy are relatively rare in this country, and in most cases have so indirect a relationship to disorders of behavior that self-medication with vitamins by persons on a reasonably adequate diet is nearly always unnecessary and may be definitely harmful.

### OTHER DRUGS

Anorexics (depressors of appetite, such as the amphetamines), aphrodisiacs (genitourinary irritants), and many other noxious substances are avidly bought by those gullible enough to believe advertisements for patent medicines or to accept misguided, subversive, or vicious advice. Nearly all such self-medications are either futile or dangerous and should be avoided.

## Convulsive Therapies

These are employed by some psychiatrists in relatively acute *psychotic* disorders, characterized, as noted, by (a) severe alterations of mood as in *depressions* or *maniacal elations,* (b) loss of contact with reality of time, place, and person, possibly with *hallucinations* (vivid imagery) or *delusions* (bizarre beliefs) as may occur in *schizophrenia,* and/or (c) *agitated behavior* dangerous to the patient or others. The common feature of these *shock therapies* is an intense physical–chemical stimulation of the brain, which causes muscular convulsions (reducible in intensity by special drugs), a transient period of coma with incomplete forgetfulness (*amnesia*) for the seizure, and progressively disorganized recall of preceding events. The biodynamic effects are therefore highly complex mixtures of interrelated physical, psychologic, and social components.

### PHYSICAL

The amnesia blunts anxious memories of recent adversities, whereas the seizures evoke adrenergic and other "body emergency" reactions that may increase alertness, mobility, and responsiveness to new experiences.

PSYCHOLOGIC

Many patients, on later reflection, vividly recall feelings of terror just before the onset of coma and during the postconvulsive state of confusion and bewilderment, and attribute their desire to "get well"—i.e., abandon their psychotic preoccupations and patterns—to this basically aversive experience. On the positive side, the induced forgetfulness of recent stresses and conflicts partially clears the way for reconsideration, reorientation, readaptation, and rehabilitation under the therapist's guidance. In addition, the re-awakening after each treatment to a welcoming audience of physician, nurse, and attendant has been characterized by some as a "symbolic rebirth" into a hopefully kindlier world.

SOCIAL

Concurrently, the hospital furnishes a haven of refuge and a general therapeutic milieu in which the patient is subjected to other predominantly favorable individual and group influences that expedite his recovery.

Since these shock therapies can be administered only by physicians with highly technical training, the methods used need be mentioned only briefly.

> *Electroshock,* achieved by passing an alternating current for a fraction of a second between electrodes generally placed on opposite temples.
>
> *Insulin* administered by intravenous injection, causing a rapid fall of blood sugar and temporary starvation of the cerebral cortex.
>
> *Indoklon* inhalations that apparently act by a combination of chemical irritation and oxygen deprivation of the brain.

All of these must be modified to fit individual cases, are always subject to complications, and are best employed in hospital or clinic settings where other therapeutic measures can be con-currently utilized. Shock therapies, at the cost of some loss of memory, conceptual ability, and latent fear and resentment, may be temporarily useful in relieving acute depressions with suicidal preoccupations; however, they effect no basic personality change unless supplemented by more dynamically reorientative, reeducative, and rehabilitative methods, and furnish no guarantee against recurrence of acute, or continuation of chronic, deviations of behavior.

## Dyadic Communicative Therapies

### PSYCHOANALYSIS

As we have seen, this term covers at least three variously interrelated concepts: (1) a method of *diagnostic investigation* (primarily through *free association, dream recall,* and *transference observation*); (2) predominantly Freudian concepts of *metapsychology*; and (3) a *therapeutic regime.* In the "classical" or "orthodox" form of the latter, the patient, with few interruptions, attends four or five fifty-minute sessions per week from two to many more years, lies on a couch facing away from the analyst, verbalizes all his current thoughts, recounts his dreams and fantasies, expresses his emotions (*v. catharsis* and *abreaction*), and discusses his attitudes (*transference*) toward the analyst. The latter, maintaining an ostensibly aloof objectivity, "interprets" all of these productions in terms of the patient's *unconscious,* his *defensive mechanisms of the ego,* his internalized *superego* prohibitions and aspirations, and his *transference relationships. Insights* so derived into the *perseveration* (persistent repetition) of *Oedipal* and *pre-Oedipal* patterns are intended to remove the patient's neurotic *fixations,* encourage new interests (*object-cathexes*), relieve his *inhibitions,* and thus permit his adult intellect to redirect his *libido* into more "mature" (i.e., more realistic, creative, socially adaptive, and ultimately satisfactory) activities. As Freud put it: "Where Id was, there shall Ego be"—although some analysands reverse this to "where Ego was, there Id shall be."

Most psychoanalysts profess to limit their clientele to patients with anxiety states, phobic–obsessive–compulsive complaints, and the milder character neuroses; others accept sociopathic personalities with rebellious, irresponsible, self-frustrating patterns of conduct, recurrent *depressives* and even so-called *ambulatory* or *pseudoneurotic schizophrenics*—essentially psychotic individuals with only a fragile veneer of adaptation to physical and cultural realities. After half a century of experience with "classical" psychoanalysis, the current consensus is that this prolonged, difficult, ritualized, and expensive mode of therapy may be instructive for professional students of the field and applicable to some carefully selected patients, but that shorter, more direct, and more versatile forms of dyadic influence are equally or more effective in most cases.

## MODIFIED ANALYTIC TECHNIQUES

Those still professedly within the analytic framework (utilizing couch, free associations, dream interpretations, etc.) stress various special aspects or objectives.

### SCHOOL OF KAREN HORNEY

Analysis is concentrated on the *social attitudes* of the patient (turning *toward, away from, or against* others) for the purpose of reestablishing individual responsibility and cultural participation. Horney eventually advocated instruction of the patient as to his social and moral duties—a modality of directiveness practiced by the late Fritz Perls in his "Gestalt therapy."

### SCHOOL OF HARRY STACK SULLIVAN

Practitioners of this subschool define psychiatry as "the study of interpersonal relationships" and undertake a minute reexamination and revision of the patient's actual normal or deviant (*parataxic*) dealings with his family, friends, and associates, as epitomized in his directly observable or inferred *social* as well as *transference transactions*. In hospital treatment a "*split transference*" may be employed by assigning the conflicting duties of permissive analyst and corrective disciplinarian to separate therapists.

SCHOOL OF FRANZ ALEXANDER

Trainees of this late, great leader in the field employ flexible schedules of interviews, daily diaries, and written records of dream series, observation and interpretation of psychosomatic correlations, frank confrontations of the patient with the analyst's appraisals of his behavior to produce *reorientative emotional experiences,* and a gradual diminution or a staggered suspension (*fractional analysis*) rather than a sudden termination of therapy.[1]

There are, of course, many other permutations and variations of theory and method among the so-called Neo-Freudian schools, but as is the case in the orthodox wing, practice often differs from precept, and results depend much more on each analyst's skill and policies than on his professed rationale.

DEVIATIONIST SCHOOLS

These were usually founded by colleagues or students of Freud who took exception to some of his basic tenets and techniques. The most prominent survivors are:

*The Individual Psychology of Alfred Adler,* which concentrates on correcting the *life style* of the patient by counteracting excessive *feelings of inferiority* and their exaggerated and impractical *overcompensations* and *masculine protests*. Therapy, reeducative and directive, is realistic in intent and pragmatic in results; peculiarly, however, Adlerian practitioners themselves tend to be unnecessarily defensive and polemic.

*The Analytic Psychology of Carl Jung* is, by contrast, preoccupied with questionable dichotomies and typologies (*logic* vs. *feeling; sensation* vs. *intuition; extrovert* vs. *introvert*), and a somewhat mystic search for a *racial unconscious* retained in an inaccessible *anima* central to one's *inner* being. Therapy, which consists in

---

[1] For an account of the author's own Alexandrian analysis, see the autobiographical *A Psychiatric Odyssey* (New York: Science House, 1970).

part of philosophic discussions and shared *intuitions* about *atavistic identifications,* is often either hortatory or nebulous.

*The approach of Otto Rank* was based on what he considered man's *primary anxiety:* the *birth trauma* consequent on the expulsion of the neonate from the Nirvana of the mother's womb into an inimical external universe. Rank's *depth analysis* was charged with providing *surrogate* or *material substitutes* for the lost securities of the embryo and was for a time popular with social workers troubled about what they considered their othewise "superficial" role; however, the Rankian and Jungian schools now have relatively few adherents in this country or elsewhere.

There are many other deviants from Freudian psychoanalysis, ranging from the disciples of Melanie Klein in Britain and South America who believe that analysis must reach down to the *primal depressions* and *paranoid states* of the first six weeks of life, to the scattered acolytes who still acccept the late Wilhelm Reich's notion that the universe is permeated by a form of *ethereal libido* that can be collected in patented *orgone boxes* for the restoration of sexual potency. As can again be inferred, therapeutic results depend far less on the theories held or rituals pursued than on the personal influences of the dedicated practitioner and the extratherapeutic securities achieved through him by his patients.

HYPNOSIS

Because of its aura of thaumaturgy and mystic power, hypnosis is perennially appealing to eager young therapists who may combine it with analytic techniques as described by Lewis R. Wolberg and others; however, objective study and disillusioning experiences (sometimes with incidentally unfortunate results for both therapist and patient) soon put the method in better perspective and properly restrict its use.

PROCEDURE

Nearly all methods of inducing the so-called *hypnnotic state* are based on (a) *selecting* a subject with conscious or unconscious wishes to undergo the experience; (b) *assaying* his influenceability by various tests such as maintaining a handclasp or swaying on suggestion; (c) providing *a restful milieu* free of distractions; (d) *reassuring* the subject as to the security and potential benefit of the procedure; (e) *reiterating simple directions* for rhythmic breathing and progressive muscular relaxations, monotonously repeated and ending in the induction of receptive drowsiness (psychophysiologically a state of concentrated attention and collaboration, and not a "trance"); and (f) *suggesting* the relief of symptoms, the recall of events, or resolutions for future action that may be accepted by the patient—or rejected by him if they are not really in accord with his own desires.

### DANGERS AND CAUTIONS

The drawbacks of hypnosis are not that patients become "submissive" and thereby subject to the will of the hypnotist like Trilby to Svengali; even in that bit of fiction Trilby repeatedly defied Svengali when it suited her to do so. The difficulties are (a) that naïve therapists themselves become deluded as to the phenomena and functions of "hypnosis" and (b) that unless the various techniques in this field [*maternal seductive, paternal authoritative, mystic,* etc. (see Masserman 1955)] are used with circumspection in carefully selected patients and only at precisely appropriate intervals in a total therapeutic program, their effects are short-lived, and complications of disappointment, suspicion, resentment, and even paranoid delusions of influence and seduction may occur. A curt aphorism of Bernheim, a pioneer and thorough student of hypnosis, applies here: There is little that can be done with hypnosis that cannot be done better, and with fewer complications, without it.

### CASE 47  Hypnotic "Regression"

Some twenty years ago, when the author was somewhat less sophisticated in the field, he had occasion to demonstrate to a class of medical students the production of "analgesia," catalepsy, automatisms and other hypnotic phenomena in an unusually cooperative eighteen-year-old patient. "Regression," too, was produced so effectively through progressively "younger age levels" that when the patient was told that she could retain her vocabulary but in every other respect must act as she had "at 2:00 p.m. on her fourth birthday," she complied by playing on the floor, and recalling in a childlike voice long-forgotten "details" (subsequently proved only remotely true) about the party she was to have later that afternoon. Suspicious of what was occurring (and I must confess, pretending to the class that I had known it all along), I then directed the patient to "relive her birth," which she did by writhing, crying, and complaining that it was "suddenly too cold and too bright!" Finally the inevitable test—on being directed to regress to "the eighth month of intrauterine life," she described her feelings in four words: "It's warm; it pulsates." But now even the most gullible student got the point: The subject, a young biology major with a strongly positive transference to the hypnotist, was doing her best, consciously or not, to comply with what she had thought the latter wanted and was using her knowledge of embryology and the birth process accordingly. In this sense, she was acting in complete accord with the concept of hypnosis she had gathered from her readings.

The "regression" in this patient is probably the earliest thus far cited in the literature, barring the "sperm memories" of Ron Hubbard dianeticians. However, equally significant is a report at the other extreme. Rubinstein and Newman noted recently that hypnotized subjects directed to live *in the future* can also describe with great vividness and seeming objectivity "events" that have not as yet occurred and are never likely to happen.

## Variations and Permutations of Therapeutic Techniques

This section covers a potpourri of methods; however, to highlight their lack of specificity, their high-sounding titles may be assembled into the question: What mode of psychiatric treatment from analysis to zootherapy (comfort in pets) does *not* "confront" the patient "sensitively" with "existence" and "reality," or is *not* "suggestive" and "client-centered," or is *not* designed to improve "behavior" through quasi-"dramatic" experiential Gestalten (*closures*) in interpersonal "transactions" intended to improve "family," "group," and "community" adaptations? Nevertheless, since avid adherents advocate them, we may consider the following cults briefly.

## EXISTENTIAL ANALYSIS

This movement has its roots in the questioning fatalism of Kierkegaard, the *fusion of subject and object* discerned by Heidegger, the *critical phenomenology* of Husserl and Binswanger, and the *Daseinanalyse* (analysis of "there it is!") of Karl Jaspers, whose watchwords are "I am; I am becoming; I am aware; I deny death." Because of its quasi-iconoclastic and intellectual appeal, the movement aroused a temporary interest in the self-styled avant-garde therapists in this country and still appeals to the abstractly philosophic-minded on the Continent. Its therapeutic theme is a simultaneous acceptance of the inevitability of death countered by a *courageous affirmation of being* (Sartre, Camus) through an appreciation of the individuality and transcendency of one's *existence*. As can be inferred, its therapy ranges from the reflectively esoteric to the defiantly erotic (*coito, ergo sum*) and is correspondingly limited in scope and effectiveness.

*Nondirective* or *Client-centered* therapy, as successively named by Carl Rogers, purports to help "clients" by providing them with a "democratic," sympathetic but noncommittal auditor for ten or so weekly sessions during which both participants can attain euthymic "self-realization"—an effect called *clearance* in Ron Hubbard's *scientology* more directly designed for the ever-numerous gullible. Whereas any friend in need in or out of office or church is better than none, most patients will prefer one more active in deed; i.e., most priests are taught to offer not only an empathic ear but more explicit directives for attaining grace after the confessional.

*Reality Therapy* (W. Glasser), *Gestalt Therapy* (F. S. Perls), and *Confrontation Therapy* (H. H. Garner): As noted, these titles, too, are tautologic, since all effective therapies "confront" the patient with the advantages of dealing holistically with conceived or misconceived physical, social and cultural "realities".

## Behavior Therapy

This is a currently popular movement ostensibly based on Pavlovian conditioning and psychologic learning theory.[1] Its techniques consist of relaxing the patient by preliminary explanations and various physical devices and then treating his inhibitions, obsessions or phobias by reassociating the object or situation feared with some correctively pleasant (sometimes sexual) experience. Conversely, the compulsive patient is forced, on pain of anxiety or actual punishment, to change his habits in favor of preferable substitutes. In essence, the three principal modalities are aversion (e.g., adding emetics to alcoholic drinks, as advocated by F. Lemere), *desensitization* (gradual reexploration of excessive aversions), and *operant reconditioning* (guided retraining). The techniques are moderately effective when applied to limited patterns of conduct that can be altered by skillful "experientially reorienting" techniques: Special claims of lasting results in serious behavior disorders, however, have not been confirmed by objective follow-up studies.

## Case 48    Reeducative Behavior Therapy of Severe Obsessive–Compulsive–Phobic Reactions

> For about five years a twenty-seven-year-old girl had developed rigid and increasingly pervasive compulsions with regard to cleanliness, dress, and diet that had finally made most of her waking hours a succession of imperative rituals. Moreover, she had such severe phobias of closed spaces, heights, the dark, and being alone on the street that in the twenty months preceding her admission to the clinics she had not dared to leave her home unescorted. The patient had a ready explanation for some of her fears. Just preceding their onset she had been followed home from work by a Negro who, she thought, "wanted to attack me," and she remembered experiencing fear

---

[1] Its attribution by J. Wolpe to my own research is based on his limited interpretations of its import.

mounting to panic *the closer to home she came.* After this episode, she had become subject to severe anxiety at theaters, dances, picnics and in a rapidly increasing number of other situations. While she admitted that some of her compulsions in hygiene and dress were not altogether justified, she defended most of them on the grounds that she had been raised by her foster-mother to be "neat," "clean," and "modest," and accordingly had developed "fixed habits" in these respects.

The girl proved to be of unusually high intelligence (IQ 142) and, despite her initial ambivalence and reserve, rapidly established a good working rapport with the therapist. A fairly rich psychiatric history was then obtained, which can be summarized as follows:

Her own parents had died when she was eight years old and she had been raised since by a married but childless aunt. The patient described this aunt as a forceful, self-reliant successful "professional woman"—a hospital head nurse—who had provided the patient with a secure home and every material need, but who had been precise and undemonstrative and had insisted on strict obedience and primly disciplined behavior in every respect. In her quest for affection the patient turned to her uncle, who also felt frustrated by his self-sufficient wife. The uncle had responded warmly, and soon became the girl's confidant and companion. However, the aunt became increasingly jealous of this attachment between her husband and niece and after the patient's menarche, had apparently begun to suspect that there was a growing erotic factor in the relationship. Accordingly, she had begun to lecture her ward on the "filthiness of sex," on the "black and benighted character of men's carnal desires," and on the necessity for continual wariness as well as righteousness on the part of all girls who would "avoid the consequences of carelessness or folly" in such matters. Concurrently, the patient's discipline became even more strict with regard to dress, habits, and demeanor until the patient herself, necessarily repressing her resentments for the sake of security, had adopted fixed rituals and persisted in them even when not under the aunt's direct supervision. Her sexual repressions became especially stringent and were manifested in an extreme modesty of dress and stilted formality of manner that further handicapped her popularity at school and her opportunities for extrafamilial activities. At college the pattern was repeated: Her intelligence and perfectionistic study habits again brought her high scholastic honors, whereas her now firmly ingrained inhibitions and social idiosyncracies prejudiced any attempt at emancipatory extracurricular and social activities.

When the patient was 19 a major crisis in her life occurred: Both her foster-parents were killed in an automobile accident. This event precipitated a period of listless depression in which, significantly, the patient could not rid herself of the obsessive idea that she had somehow been responsible for the accident, and particularly for the death of her aunt. So disturbing was this thought that she abandoned school, made no effort to share in her aunt's estate, went to live with another relative, and soon afterward took a routine, underpaid job as a government secretary. She continued to be exact but inefficiently slow in her work and inhibited in her social relations, although apparently she had no serious difficulties until the threatened "attack" by the Negro. After this, however, frank episodes of anxiety appeared, and her phobias, obsessions, and compulsions increased rapidly as recounted above.

THERAPY

At first, the patient was permitted to indulge all of her idiosyncracies in the ward: wearing voluminously concealing pajamas and robes even in bed, remaining isolated in her room, rinsing each dish before eating from it, washing her hands every half-hour and so on. No immediate attempt was made to investigate or interpret these defenses but, as rapport was gained in succeeding interviews, it was noteworthy that the patient herself began to recognize the meanings of some of them and to discontinue others spontaneously. For instance, she began to correlate her fear of dirt with her extreme inhibitions "about dirty sexual thoughts" and finally began to recognize and confess that she had felt these inhibitions to be necessary not only because they had been ingrained by severe training but because they were counterreactions to her own erotic wishes. These she continued for a time to characterize merely as "filthy ideas," but gradually she added more specific content. For instance, she recollected that during high school she had attempted digital masturbation, had suffered reactions of severe guilt, and had been so obsessed with the idea that her hands smelled of vaginal secretion that she had developed "a habit of washing them before touching anything anyone else might touch." In this connection, too, she hinted that the very act of rubbing her hands in thick soap was in some respects itself a symbolic form of displaced masturbation. Similarly, she admitted that her anxiety during the episode of the Negro was less fear of injury than a horrified fascination with the idea of a forced intercourse for which she could not be held responsible and a growing impulse to permit herself to be "raped by a black man in the dirty alley right by my aunt's house—so the closer I got there *the more afraid of my aunt* I became."

The patient was, of course, amazed that such confessions were anticipated and taken as a matter of course, and for a time she could not accept the therapist's assurances that they did not indicate her complete depravity. Nevertheless, in the security of the therapeutic situation the patient's tolerance to reorientation gradually increased, and, as her anxieties and guilts diminished, her transference needs became more spontaneous explicit and therapeutically useful. For instance, the patient began to envy the "privileges" other patients were granted by the therapist, such as coming to his office for interviews, being permitted to take walks outside the hospital, eating in a common dining-room, etc. Accordingly, she began to emulate these activities first with the companionship of a nurse, and eventually alone; indeed, within two weeks after her admission the patient was attending the theater in "afternoons off" from the hospital. At this point, moreover, her energies could be turned into constructive and rehabilitative channels. She was asked to volunteer part-time services as an aide in one of the clinical laboratories of the hospital. As was anticipated, her previous "fears" of excreta also had their strongly attractive aspects, and the patient became highly intriqued with the technique of urinalysis, blood counts, and such other symbolically voyeuristic pursuits. Moreover, because of her intelligence and precision, she rapidly proved herself to be a valuable assistant. Plans were therefore worked out for her to take up this training professionally, and the patient, while still hospitalized, was sent to a downtown laboratory to apply as a student helper—a position that she secured almost entirely on her own initiative. During the fourth and last week of her hospitalization, she was seen frequently by a social worker whose offers to aid and accompany her in finding social and recreational outlets were accepted and utilized. In this way, the momentum of the patient's recovery was carried over after her discharge from the hospital, and she not only began to work at an interesting and promising career, but also expanded her social contacts through the medium of YWCA activities, volunteer Red Cross work, study clubs, etc. Her readaptations were at first guided by interviews every few weeks with the psychiatrist and social worker, but within a year these seemed no longer necessary. At a follow-up interview three years after her discharge the patient reported that she had completed her training, received a technician's certificate, and was steadily employed in a hospital laboratory. She still had some tendencies toward compulsive orderliness of habits, but her disruptive phobias, obsessions, and compulsions had almost completely disappeared. She had cultivated friends and recreational interests, had become engaged to a man after a mutually satisfactory sexual liaison with him, and she anticipated with pleasure their marriage on his return from service overseas.

COMMENT

For the sake of accuracy, it may be well to point out that the dynamisms of the patient's recovery were not as rationalistic as appeared on the surface. Various dream-associations and other material indicated that on deeply unconscious levels the therapy had in large part been effective because the patient had formed a pseudo-avuncular transference to the therapist, and that in this relationship she had recapitulated various childhood rivalries and identifications in emulating the patterns of the other patients. Finally, in adopting the work of a laboratory technician, the patient had not only acted out the obverse of her fears of "dirt," but had unconsciously identified herself with the professional standing of her aunt under the aegis of another aunt-surrogate, the social worker. When this identification was not only permitted but encouraged in the therapy, she could express her previously repressed erotic and other drives with markedly decreased anxiety—although, of course, in a relatively sublimated and socially acceptable fashion. In this sense, the patient was still partially "neurotic"—and yet this very utilization of neurotic dynamisms for desirable personal and social reorientations represents a therapeutic artifice useful in many modes of therapy to produce the desired effects.

## TRANSACTIONAL THERAPIES

These are usually associated with the "personality structure" and "game" concepts of Eric Berne, here summarized: Every person may assume an *extero-*, a *neo-*, or an *arche-psychic* "Ego state," roughly corresponding in analytic terminology to Superego, Ego, and Id, respectively. Accordingly, he may conduct himself as a Parent (nurturing, authoritative, or punitive), as an Adult (realistic, forethoughtful, adaptational), or as a Child (subservient, free, or reckless). Two persons, when transactionally "hooked," can thereby interact variously in *Parent ⇌ Child, Adult ⇌ Adult,* or *Child ⇌ Adult vectors,* each with almost an infinity of derived nuances at various psychological or social, "open" or "locked" levels. The resulting transactions (see Stephen Potter's *How to Win Without Actually Cheating*) may in their turn be whimsically categorized as: *Why Don't You. . . . Yes But* (mutual frustration), *Uproar* (chaos), *Alcoholic* (I can't help my metabolic disease), *Wooden Leg* or *Schlemiel* (I'm very sorry I'm so awkward), *Pirhana* (everyone strip the flesh off one victim), *PTA* (parents against teachers against pupils and vice versa), and so on. Another frequent triangle with double arrows in all three directions is named by Stephen Karpman *Persecutor ⇌ Rescuer ⇌ Victim ⇌ Persecutor.* These games are segments of more complex and enduring patterns called *scripts,* which constitute each person's overall life plan and are used for the following purposes:

a.    To *reaffirm a position* (e.g., "All men are beasts").
b.    To *collect trading stamps* (e.g., *brown*—"I am hurt and sulky"; *blue*—"Don't I feel guilty enough already?"; *red*—"I

have every right to be angry"; or *gray*—"You're driving me insane"). Accumulated "books of stamps" are traded in for presumed social gains.

c.  To *get strokes*—i.e., handicap the opponents in the "game."
d.  To *stretch time* through various delays and rituals.
e.  And generally to *advance the script* by playing Cinderella, Ulysses, Oedipus, *et al*.

Such transactions may be exposed, interpreted and counteracted in both dyadic or group sessions by the therapist or his surrogates. Groups are generally kept small (eight to twelve) and may be entered only after each participant has clearly designated his therapeutic objectives and agreed to a formal *contract* (e.g., he must keep his job, control his drinking, adhere to the group mores, etc.). Meetings are held once or twice weekly and may be supplemented by individual interviews, designated readings, and ancillary assignments. Berne and his trainees claim comparatively favorable and enduring results, and may well secure them in relatively intelligent, well-integrated, and transactionally mobile patients whose prognosis had been rendered all the more favorable from the beginning by their possession of a sense of self-evaluative humor.

OTHER GROUP THERAPIES

These utilize the salutary influences of group leadership, participation in common endeavors and the attendant development of interpersonal rapport, sympathetic understanding, and mutual helpfulness—all particularly valuable in the treatment of isolated, alienated individuals. Typical forms and techniques of group therapy include:

*Discussion groups,* composed usually of six to ten patients, led by one or two therapists or selected participants who meet regularly to explore the relevance to their lives of current events, individual experiences, and the special or conjoint needs of the participants.

*Psychodrama* (Moreno) is a variant in which patients *act out* scenes from their past or anticipated future, using therapists or other patients as *auxiliary egos* to play important personages in these episodes. Roles are then mimicked (*mirror or double technique*), changed, or reversed in order to broaden the subject's understanding of how his behavior appears to others. When skillfully conducted, the method may be illuminating, but care must be taken to avoid excessive histrionics and to keep clear for both patient and therapist the distinctions between the fantasies of wishful play-acting and the realities of present and future existence.

*Family therapy* limits the group to related members, whose interactions are observed, elucidated, and presumably improved in successive sessions with one or more therapists.

*Music, dance, painting, vocational,* and other such group therapies utilize these respective aesthetic and manipulative modalities to stimulate activity, cultivate common interests, and encourage creative social expressions.

*Esalen, Training* (T), *Sensitivity, Nudity,* and other such recently mushrooming cults, advocate a variety of other esoteric, regressive, or erotic forms of "group encounter," with correspondingly greater dangers of exceeding essential individual and group restraints and reality adaptations during and especially after such experiences—sometimes with unfortunate results.

*Alcoholics Anonymous* is an organization that specializes in helping alcoholics by combinations of ever-ready *rescue services,* temporary economic aid, fraternal persuasion, and religious exhortation; among suitable subjects, it claims about 50 percent improvement.

A corresponding endeavor called *Synanon* deals with narcotic addicts, with equivocal results to date. *Daytop* in New York and various branches of *Synanon* have expanded their activities to provide shelter and intensive programs of social and occupational rehabilitation not only to drug addicts but to other marginal misfits who sincerely deserve help.

The *Mattachine Society* and *Recovery, Inc.,* are national organizations whose members are concerned respectively with the privileges and welfare of homosexuals and of formerly hospitalized mental patients.

## Community Psychiatry

Various aspects of this field have already been discussed under the rubric of community care for the psychotic and aged. However, as it becomes more generally accepted that just as the community is charged with the prevention and treatment of infectious diseases, so also is it responsible for preventing behavior disorders or caring for them in their earliest, more treatable stages, the following services will be provided:

1.  *Counseling for students and teachers* in the school systems from kindergarten through college, with special attention to actual or potential scholastic failures, premature dropouts, teen-age pregnancies, and the growing problems of drug abuse and delinquency.
2.  *Consultation services for police,* welfare, and other federal, state, and municipal departments as to internal personnel policies as well as programs that affect social cohesion, security, and morale.
3.  *Out-patient clinics and more specialized suicide prevention centers* to which persons in desperate straits and suffering extreme despondency can appeal at any hour for immediate hope and interim aid.
4.  *Day hospitals* designed for the individual and group treatment of patients who would benefit by continued contact with their home and family.
5.  *Night hospitals* that furnish evening and nighttime therapy for patients while they are kept beneficially employed.
6.  *Wards in general hospitals* where patients requiring full-time

care can be admitted for short periods without the onus of legal proceedings.

7. *Community zone centers* as developed in Illinois and New York in which all of these services are combined with research and teaching leading to further progress.

8. *Prolonged treatment hospitals* for more serious or chronic illnesses, some of which may require court commitment of the patient.

## Inferences, and Conclusions

If patients are to continue to come at all for the comprehensive care they seek, therapists must cherish and increase the regard the public has for them not only as skilled technicians but as dedicated humanitarians deserving the highest respect and confidence. Differences of professional opinion, as in any scientific field, are acceptable, but we must face the dilemma that, of late, public polemics, a trade-union image, and sometimes blatant economic and political partisanships have diminished and impaired the trust medical and other therapists must inspire if they are to serve patients to their best advantage.

Next, therapists must discard the cold armor of aloof "professional dignity" and accept each supplicant not as a "diagnostic challenge" or as a subject for stereotyped therapy—and least of all as only another research datum—but as a *troubled human being seeking relief and guidance.* Bodily discomforts and dysfunctions are to be alleviated by every means available, with the aid of medical and other consultations as necessary. As soon as the patient's tensions and anxieties have abated sufficiently to make him more accessible and cooperative, every effort must be made to revoke his initiative, restore his strength and lost skills (Ur-need I), and encourage him to regain the confidence and self-respect that can come only from useful accomplishment.

Concurrently, since "no man is an Iland, intire of itselfe," the wise therapist, whatever his speciality, has a broader task: to recognize that his patient may be deeply concerned about sexual, marital, occupational, and other problems that can also seriously affect his physical and social well-being. This involves an exploration, varying in depth and duration but always discerning and tactful, of the attitudes and values the patient derived from his past experiences, his present goals and tribulations, his effective (normal), culturally ineffective (neurotic), or bizarrely unrealistic (psychotic) conduct, the ways in which these patterns relieve or exacerbate his current difficulties, and whether they are accessible to various methods of medicopsychologic therapy. With consultation as needed, in many cases a properly trained, intelligent, sensitive, and dedicated nonmedical therapist can conduct the therapy required. In essence, this will consist of using gentle reasoning, personal guidance, and progressive social explorations to help the patient correct his past misconceptions and prejudices, abandon infantile or childlike patterns of behavior that have long since lost their effectiveness, revise his goals and values, and adopt a more realistic, productive, and lastingly rewarding ("mature") style of life. In this skillfully directed reeducation (good psychotherapy, despite recent fads to the contrary, is about as "nondirective" as good surgery), the enlightened cooperation of his family, friends, employer, or others may, with the patient's consent, be secured and utilized to the full. By such means the patient's second Ur-need will be met through renewed communal solidarity and security—*a sine qua non* of comprehensive treatment.

Finally, and to mitigate the third Ur-anxiety, the patient's religious, philosophic, or other convictions, instead of being deprecated or undermined, should be respected and strengthened insofar as they furnish him with what each of us requires: a belief in life's purpose, meaning, and value. To repeat: Psychology, psychiatry, and the other humanitarian sciences can never be in conflict with philosophy or religion, since all are designed by a beneficent providence to preserve, cheer, and comfort man; they thereby constitute a trinity to be respected by any therapist deeply concerned with man's health and sanity.

## History Teaches That History Cannot Teach Us —and Yet . . .

With so many consistencies between past and present, can we dare to extrapolate the future? Let us group a few predictions around our now familiar categories.

### SURVIVAL

In accord with the perennial legends of Pandora, Golem, Franken-stein *et al.* in almost every mythology, we now have at hand enough nuclear bombs to kill every man, woman, and child on earth twenty times over, plus the knowledge that even if they remain unexploded, unless drastic measures are taken to reverse pollution and overpopulation, there is more than one chance in three that *homo habilis* will perish by the year 2000. Even if we survive but persist too arduously in our frenetic quest for scientific and technical mastery, we shall discover dimensions and forces yet unconceived but perhaps better not known; we shall distill the ocean and desiccate its fish for tasteless food; we shall conquer cancer and produce new diseases; we shall explore the planets and find them globular hells; and we shall continue to be more bewildered and frustrated than ever by the endless and inscrutable cosmos. And yet we must participate in the unquenchable optimism of our race and trust that, even so, our progeny will somehow also survive.

### UR-SOCIETY IN THE FUTURE

A world community is the only alternative to Armageddon, and since *homo habilis* is a single, universally fecund species, differ-ences of race or color will eventually become about as indistinguish-able as Lombard, Hittite, or Etruscan strains now are in their mixed Mediterranean descendants. The inhabitants of this earth will certainly become more alike and, out of sheer necessity, increasingly friendly and cooperative.

### UR-THEOLOGY OF THE FUTURE

If so, men will develop a deeper sense of purposive existence that will transcend the symbolic legends, rituals, and theocracies of our current religions farther than we have progressed from the animistic worship of our barbaric ancestors. When we achieve this breadth of vision and depth of understanding, we may also become wiser, humbler, kinder—and perhaps a bit happier. Here, however, a final contrapuntal reflection may be in order: Since all man's perceptions and derived concepts are essentially subjective, why, after all, call the beliefs we have here considered Ur-"illusions," since we live and shall continue to live by them?

## Résumé

In review, then, man's ultimate (Ur-) anxieties are three: first, his abhorrence of physical injury and death; second, his uncertainty as to the reliability of his human alliances; third, his utter rejection of the thought that perhaps he is, after all, little more than a cosmic triviality. It is equally significant that these triple trepidations of man also motivate his principal modes of presumed mastery. His maneuvers are here again, three: first, his attempt to subjugate his material milieu through various sciences and technologies, including medicine (Ur-defense I); next, his efforts to guarantee his social relationships by familial, economic, and political compacts (Ur-hope II); and finally, his endeavors to encompass the entire universe in his philosophic and religious systems (Ur-faith III). Unfortunately, as we know, his strivings in all of these modalities often fail, whereupon he becomes our impatient patient and calls upon us as physicians, counselors, and ministers to serve him in corresponding modes of therapy. These, predictably, are again tripartite: first, the restoration of his bodily strengths and skills; second, the recultivation of human companionships; and third, the reinvocation of his transcendent beliefs and protective gods. Can any mortal therapist do more?

# Glossary of Essential Psychologic and Psychiatric Terms

The following basic definitions, worded as simply and meaningfully as possible, will help clarify and supplement the text:

AFFECT. Generalized feeling tone, usually distinguished from emotion in being more persistent and pervasive, less directly reflected in physiologic deviations, and with more generalized ideational content.

AFFECTIVE PSYCHOSES. Psychoses (see p. 56 ff.) characterized prominently by marked changes in mood; e.g., *depression* or *mania*.

ALZHEIMER'S DISEASE. A generalized fibrillary degeneration of the cerebral cortex with glial plaque formation occurring in late middle life and manifested by a variable but usually rapidly progressive symptomatology comprising *aphasia*, *apraxia*, intellectual deterioration, habit disintegration, explosiveness of affect, and, occasionally, convulsive seizures.

AMBIVALENCE. Incompatibility of simultaneous attitudes, generally unconscious, with regard to alternative possibilities of action, e.g., mixed love and hate for the same person.

AMENTIA. Lack of development of intellectual capacities.

AMNESIA. Loss of memory or recall. *Anterograde a.* signifies forgetfulness for events following some trauma, such as cerebral concussion or an epileptic seizure, as distinguished from *retrograde a.*, or loss of memory for events preceding such traumata. *Lacunar* or *patchy a.* connotes an inability to recall specific events or portions of them, with preserved memory for episodes between them.

ANXIETY. A state of apprehensive tension that arises during motivational and adaptational conflicts. Anxiety is experienced in circumstances of direct or symbolic danger, or when phobic, compulsive, or other accustomed defenses are transgressed.

ANXIETY SYNDROME. The physiologic concomitants of anxiety, generally experienced as palpitation (consciousness of racing or pounding heart); shallow, rapid, or constricted respiration; globus (sensations of tightness or a lump in the throat); trembling; "fluttering" in the abdomen; sweaty, flushed, or pale skin; and subjective diffuse apprehensiveness that may mount to feelings of impending catastrophe and panic. Incontinence may occur in severe attacks.

APHASIA. Impairment of communicative functions. *Sensory* or *impressive* aphasia includes inability to perceive auditory, tactile, or visual speech-symbols; semantic aphasia denotes impaired recall (amnestic a.), recognition (anomia), or correlation (syntactic a., *aphasia*) of speech symbols; *motor expressive aphasia* indicates a loss of verbal, written, or mimetic speech expression. These types of aphasia are all present in varying degree in *organic* aphasia and, when complete, constitute *global* aphasia. In functional or neurotic aphasia one or several specific dysfunctions may appear in relative isolation.

ASSOCIATION, FREE. 1. The psychoanalytic technique of requiring the patient to express or describe all thoughts, sensations, and emotions as they occur during the analytic hour. 2. The *verbalizations* so elicited.

AURA. Sensations or other prodromal experiences (sometimes hallucinatory) that regularly or irregularly precede each episode of a paroxysmal disorder, e.g., migraine or epilepsy.

AUTOMATISM. Mechanical, repetitive, apparently undirected, symbolic behavior, often without conscious control, seen in *fugue states* or *schizophrenia*.

AUTONOMIC NERVOUS SYSTEM. That portion of the nervous system that regulates the glands, circulation, and internal organs. Its *parasympathetic* (craniosacral) division is, in general, anabolic and inhibitory; its *orthosympathetic* (thoracolumbar) division is in general catabolic and excitatory, but (a) there are specific exceptions in organ-innervation, and (b) the two divisions are intimately interactive.

BEHAVIORISM. A system of psychology (J. B. Watson) that studies the conduct and therapy (J. Wolpe) of human beings exclusively on the principle of association and professes to exclude consciousness and other subjective and conative considerations as irrelevant epiphenomena.

BIODYNAMICS. The historical, comparative and experimental study of the dynamic processes manifested in the behavior of organisms.

CASTRATION COMPLEX. In psychoanalytic theory, fear of traumatic degenitalization in either sex as punishment for forbidden erotic desires. The term, however, has been used with a variety of connotations ranging from fear of literal castration (Freud) to symbolic deprivation of any cherished possession.

CATAPLEXY. A sudden, passing attack of muscular weakness with or without loss of consciousness. May occur in conjunction with *narcolepsy*.

CATASTROPHIC REACTIONS. Severe disintegration of behavior under excessive stress, especially in patients whose adaptive capacities are impaired by cerebral injury (K. Goldstein).

CATATONIA. A clinical form of schizophrenia (see p. 157) characterized by motor disturbances (hyperactivity, rigidity, or, rarely, flexibilitias cerea), stupor, occasional marked excitement, and a relatively acute or episodic course.

CATHARSIS. The partial dissipation of the morbid residua of a repressed traumatic experience by therapeutic verbalization or acting-out, accompanied by emotional discharge or abreaction. This occurs during psychoanalytic therapy, or it may be induced by hypnosis (*hypnocatharsis*) or drugs (*narcoanalysis*), with or without interpretation and guided retraining by the therapist (*narcosynthesis*)—a form of rapid therapy often effective in acute combat neuroses.

CATHEXIS. In psychoanalysis, "libidinal charge," or investment of an object or idea with special significance or value-tone for the individual, e.g., individualized love, hatred, or ambivalent combinations of affect with reference to a thing or person.

CHARACTER. The interrelated patterns of behavior of an individual; distinguished by some from *personality* in that the latter may mean more specifically the *social* manifestations of character patterns.

COMPLEX, INFERIORITY. In Adlerian *individual psychology*, unconscious feelings of inferiority or inadequacy stemming from excessive disciplinary subordination or physical inadequacies (*organ inferiority*) in childhood, for which the individual may try to overcompensate by excessive ambitiousness, aggressiveness, domination, or special accomplishment to overcome the handicap.

COMPLEX, OEDIPUS. In early psychoanalytic theory, the erotic attachment of the child to the parent of the opposite sex, repressed because of the fear of *castration* (see p. 78) by the jealous parent. [From the Greek myth in which Laius, King of Thebes, exiles his infant son Oedipus, who is rescued by a shepherd. Later Oedipus in his wanderings unknowingly kills his father and marries Jocasta, his mother. Whᵉ ⸱ he discovers this, he blinds (symbolically castrates) himself but is later pardoned by the Fates.]

COMPULSION. An act carried out (despite some professed rejection and resistance by the patient) in accordance with a persistent idea (obsession), and in order to avoid inexplicable anxiety should the impulse not be followed.

CONDENSATION. A symbolic process by which many concepts may be represented by one. For instance, in symbolic imagery a snake may represent phallic erotism, slinking danger, low bestiality, pitiless aggressivity, mystic fascination, etc. So, too, a *phobia* or a *conversion symptom* may condense and represent in compromise form many otherwise incompatible symbolizations and adaptations.

CONDITIONING. In Pavlovian *reflexology* and Watsonian *behaviorism*, the process by which innate responses ("unconditioned reflexes"), when associated with new sensory stimuli, may thereafter be evoked by these stimuli acting alone.

CONFABULATION. A tendency to substitute detailed but fantastic, inconsistent, and variable accounts—each version currently believed by the patient during its telling—to fill in gaps of memory produced by organic cerebral disease [e.g., as in alcoholic (*Korsakoff*) or *senile* psychoses].

CONVERSION. In psychoanalytic theory, the process whereby sexual libido is "converted" and redirected into bodily (*autoplastic*) aberrations of behavior. The term is now mainly used to designate *hysterical* sensorimotor dysfunctions such as blindness or paralysis.

COUNTERTRANSFERENCE. 1. In psychoanalytic theory, the symbolic libidinal relationships, partly unconscious, of the analyst with the analytic patient (*analysand*) that may impair the ideal objectivity of the analytic process. 2. In general, the therapist's attitudes toward the patient, based on the former's interpersonal evaluations of the latter.

CRIMINALITY. Asocial, antisocial, or illegal conduct that, nevertheless, is in accordance with the conscious standards and intent of the individual. Theoretically, though not always practically, distinguishable from (1) *neurotic* or sociopathic behavior, in which the aberrant conduct is deviantly symbolic rather than indulged in for extrinsic gain, and (2) from *psychotic* behavior in which excesses of uncontrollable affect or distortions of generally accepted reality occasion the antisocial act.

CYCLOTHYMIA. A tendency to persistent, irrational, or exaggerated shifts in mood, especially with regard to alternations of *euphoria* (*hypomania, mania*) and *depression* (hypothymia, melancholia).

DEFENSE MECHANISM. 1. In psychoanalytic theory, a process by which the *Ego* (the orientative and integrative portion of the personality) partially satisfies the unconscious drives of the instinctive *Id* by behavior that conforms with the self-regulative demands of the *Superego* (see pp. 142 and 162). 2. In general, adaptive modes of behavior constituting compromises among the needs of the organism and its experientially contingent apperceptions and evaluations of its milieu.

DELINQUENCY. Asocial, antisocial, illegal, or culturally nonconforming conduct in a minor.

DELIRIUM. In modern usage, a state of disorientation and confusion (often with rapidly changing, generally fearful hallucinations), induced by the toxic effects of organic diseases or drugs (e.g., alcoholic *delirium tremens*).

DELUSION. A fixed belief widely deviant from the cultural norm and impervious to persuasion or reason.

DEMENTIA. Deterioration of perceptive, integrative, and manipulative (e.g., "intellectual") capacities due to organic disease of the brain.

DEMENTIA, SCHIZOPHRENIC. A term referring to the supposed "mental degeneration" in schizophrenia. Actually, however, there is only disinterest in, and abandonment, disuse, or distortion of, complex intellectual and social processes, but no demonstrable deterioration of capacities (*dementia*) occurs unless secondary organic cerebral changes supervene as a result of the patient's physical debility or intercurrent diseases.

DENIAL. In psychoanalysis, an unconscious *defense* whereby the patient refuses to recognize or accept unwelcome conations or concepts.

DEPERSONALIZATION. A subject's feeling or belief that he has lost his identity. Is evanescent in *hypnogogic states* or in neurotic reactions, but may be persistent and accompanied by cosmic delusions in the psychoses.

DEPRESSION. A state characterized effectively by maintained dejection in mood, ideologically by gloomy ruminations or forebodings, and physiologically by the depressive syndrome (see below). Depressions range in intensity and persistence from evanescent "blues" to deep *melancholia*. See *psychoses, depressive*.

DEPRESSION, REACTIVE. A self-limited affective state, the content, intensity, and duration of which have rational reference to "actual" rather than "symbolic" frustrations, deprivations, or adversities in the life of the patient. Distinguished from *psychosis* by the criteria listed under the latter (see below).

DEPRESSION-SYNDROME, PHYSIOLOGIC. Depressive states are typically accompanied by varying degrees of anorexia, loss of weight, constipation or other gastrointestinal dysfunctions, easy fatigability, and diminished sexual desire. In women, disturbances of menstruation are common; in men, relative impotence. Energy is generally decreased, so that ideation and action are slowed, but diurnal variations (morning retardation, partially dispelled toward evening) may occur. However, there may be episodes of markedly increased appetite (*bulimia*); or a persistent, aimless, motor restlessness (*agitation*) may supervene.

DEREISM. Unreal, delusional conduct, i.e., not in accordance with generally accepted interpretations of space, time, and logic. Generally applied to schizophrenic fantasies and their "irrational" organization.

DETERIORATION. 1. Degeneration of intellectual capacities due to organic cerebral disease (e.g., alcoholic d., senile d.), as manifested by variable *amnesias, aphasias, apraxias,* disturbances of category formation, impairment of energy (*power factor*), or loss of other intellectual functions.

DIAGNOSIS. Determination of the nature and intensity of a morbid process or processes. In modern psychiatry, diagnosis entails a balanced survey of the nature, context, and extent of all significant behavioral aberrations, as distinguished from mere superficial classification by "disease entities" (*taxonomy, nosology*).

DISPLACEMENT. The transfer of symbolic meaning and value from one object or concept to another: E.g., a mother may cherish a pet excessively after her child's death; a man may redirect unconscious hate of his father onto his boss; or a girl may conceal displaced concern over her genital functions in obsessive–compulsive oral hygiene.

DISSOCIATION. 1. The severance of normal relationships and sequences among conations, thoughts, ..id affects. 2. Complex combinations of behavior patterns that, though integrated among themselves, may appear unrelated to the rest of the personality, giving rise to *double* or *multiple personality* (Prince) or to *encapsulated paranoia* (Bleuler).

DISTORTION. An adaptive alteration of a perception or concept to conform with the subject's wishes or prejudices, e.g., a distorted apperception and evaluation of the personality characteristics of a loved or hated person.

DREAM-FUNCTION. In psychoanalytic theory, a process by which dream fantasies express unconscious wishes and reexplore and allay anxieties through symbolic representation and resolution.

ECONOMICS. 1. In dynamic psychiatry, the study of the respective weighting, interaction, and balance of adaptive processes to produce final behavior. 2. In psychoanalytic theory, the distribution of *libido* according either to the *pleasure-principle*, the *psychosexual development* or the *death-instincts*.

EGO. In psychoanalytic theory, that portion or stratum of the "mind" or personality that is in contact with the environment through the senses, perceives and evaluates the milieu through intellectual functions, and directs behavior into acceptable compromises between the blind drives of the *Id* and the inhibitions (conscience) and idealizations (*Ego-ideal*) of the *Superego* (see p). 216-217).

EGO-ANALYSIS. In psychoanalysis, the investigation of the methods (*defenses*) by which the *Ego* (a) resolves conflicts among *Id* drives or between these and *Superego* inhibitions, thus averting disruptive anxiety, and (b) adapts by "normal" or "neurotic" mechanisms to the demands of reality as conceptually interpreted.

EGO-IDEAL. In psychoanalytic theory, that portion or function of the Superego that orientates and directs the personality toward ends and goals—usually those of other persons with whom the subject has, in the past, identified his own interests.

EIDETIC IMAGERY. Vivid, detailed, accurate, voluntarily controllable recall of previous sensory impressions, reported to be present in 60 percent of children and in some adults (see *types*, Jaensch).

ELECTROSHOCK THERAPY. A form of treating psychiatric disorders by passing an electric current through the brain, usually with the induction of convulsions and coma.

EMOTION. A state of excitation manifested during conative press or conflicts and reflected in characteristic physiologic reactions and motor expressions.

EMPATHY. The "objective" or "intellectual" recognition of the nature and significance of another's behavior, as distinguished from sympathy, derived from corresponding conative and effective experiences.

EPICRITIC SENSITIVITY. Accurate appreciation of light touch, temperature, and point-to-point distance on the skin, distinguished from grosser *protopathic* sensations of pain or pressure (Head).

EPILEPSY. A group of disorders characterized mainly by motor convulsions and/or disturbances of consciousness, often traceable by electroencephalography to cerebral dysrhythmias; generally episodic, except in the *continuous partial epilepsy* of Wilson and in *status epilepticus*. Distinguished from toxic convulsions and hysterical seizures in etiology, course, and prognosis. See *epilepsy*, *major*.

EPILEPSY, JACKSONIAN. Recurrent convulsive movements beginning in one extremity and accompanied by minimal disturbances of consciousness. These may arise from circumscribed cerebral lesions (Hughlings Jackson).

EPILEPSY, MAJOR (GRAND MAL). Typically, episodic disturbances or abolition of consciousness, with tonic contractions rapidly involving the whole body (*opisthotonos*) followed by violent *clonic* movements during which there may be urinary or fecal incontinence. The attack may be heralded by a *prodromal aura* (sensory, affective, or hallucinatory experiences) and the convulsions may be immediately preceded by an explosive epileptic cry. If the patient is not prepared for the seizure he generally falls and may bite his tongue or injure himself during the convulsions. *Postdromata* often consist of lassitude, muscular weakness or soreness, headache, and amnesia for the seizure. Epilepsy may be distinguished from toxic convulsive states (e.g., strychnine, tetany, and hysterical seizures by its etiology, symptoms, and course.

EPILEPSY, MINOR (PETIT MAL). Epilepsy characterized by relatively mild muscular movements or sometimes only by momentary impairments of consciousness (*absences* during which the patient may automatically continue his previous activity) (minor epileptic fugue).

EPILEPTIC CHARACTER. Thought by some to comprise personality traits of intense affective ambivalence, obsessive–compulsive tendencies, hypersensitivity, mysticism and religiosity, and a propensity for vacillating instability between extremes of impulsive behavior. However, it is probable that the concept of an "epileptic character type" has no independent validity, and, in the relatively few patients in whom such traits are marked, they represent secondary neurotic reactions to the epileptic disorder rather than a correlated constitutional deviation.

EPILEPTIC EQUIVALENT. Any episodic sensory, motor, or experiential phenomena that may replace convulsive seizures in epilepsy (see *psychic epilepsy*).

EPILEPTIC FUGUE. A state of disturbed, clouded, bewildered, or dreamlike consciousness with integrated but automatic and occasionally violent activity following epileptic seizures.

The fugue may persist from minutes to (in rare cases) days and is thereafter generally submerged in almost complete *amnesia*.

EPILEPTIC STATUS. Incessant or nearly continuous epileptic seizures that, in extreme cases, may lead to exhaustion and death if not therapeutically controlled.

EPINOSIC GAIN. Secondary advantages derived from an illness or behavior disorder, as distinguished from the essential *paranosic* determinants and phenomena of the illness itself.

EXTINCTION. The disappearance of a *conditioned reflex* (Pavlov) when it is repeatedly elicited without reinforcement by the *unconditioned reflex* through the provision of a reward.

EXTROVERSION. Interest and participation in the "external" world, as distinguished from *introversion*, or preoccupation with endogenous, "self-centered" fantasies and *autistic* behavior (Jung).

FIXATION. 1. The persistence of a definite goal or pattern of behavior. 2. In psychoanalytic theory, the continuation into later life of some pregenital (e.g., oral or anal) phase of interest in, or evaluation of, objects (*libidinal cathexis*).

FUGUE. A state in which the patient's consciousness and behavior, though they may be well integrated, show an apparent break in continuity with previous patterns. Epileptic fugues (see p. 201) leave an almost complete amnesia for their duration; *hysterical* fugues leave a lacunar and generally penetrable amnesia.

GRANDIOSITY. Delusions of being wealthy, famous, powerful, omniscient, etc.

GUILT. Conscious or unconscious dread of loss of love or retributive punishment for impulses or deeds forbidden in earlier experiences.

HALLUCINATION. An auditory, visual, tactile (haptic) or other apperception accepted as real by the subject but occasioned by no apparent external sensory stimuli. Hallucinations differ from *hypnagogic* or dream imagery in that no corrective reorientation occurs immediately after the imagery ceases, or on waking. On the other hand, the rapidly changing, fearful hallucinations of toxic deliria are recognized by the patient to have been unreal after his recovery.

HOMEOSTASIS. The tendency of organisms to maintain their metabolic processes in so far as possible within optimal limits for individual and race survival (Bernard, Cannon).

HYPNOSIS (HYPNOTISM). A trance-like passive state produced by monotonous, reiterated suggestion of relaxation, sleep, and control by the hypnotist, in which the subject shows increased amenability and responsiveness to directions or commands, provided that these do not conflict seriously with the subject's own conscious or unconscious wishes. "Forgotten" memories may be recalled, and altered states of sensibility, perception, or motor function may be induced. Acceptable acts may also be compulsively performed by the subject after the *hypnotic trance* has been terminated (*posthypnotic suggestion*), and the patient may profess a directed forgetfulness for his experiences during the trance (posthypnotic *amnesia*).

HYSTERIA. 1. A state of neurotic sensorimotor dysfunction, e.g., hysterical blindness, paralysis, or convulsions. 2. A lay term for great emotional and motor excitation ("hysterics") should not be used in this sense in psychiatric description or diagnosis.

ID. In psychoanalytic theory, a general term for all unconsciously determined instincts or libidinal strivings (see p. 205), constituting the conative "portion" of the personality.

IDENTIFICATION. Wishful adoptions, mainly unconscious, of the personality characteristics or identity of another individual, generally one possessing advantages that the subject envies and desires.

IDIOCY, MORAL (MORAL INSANITY OF PRICHARD). Almost obsolete terms connoting a serious lack of "moral sense" or "moral development," i.e., the inadequate establishment of social responsibilities and adaptations. Contrast criminality and psychopathy.

ILLUSION. A misinterpretation of a sensory percept, usually fleeting or correctable by closer or supplementary examination of the external stimulus.

IMBECILITY. General intellectual deficiency such that the average intelligence level is between about one-quarter and one-half normal. Imbeciles nearly always require institutional care.

INHIBITION. 1. In general, the internal checking or restraint of a *conation*, *affect*, thought or act. 2. In psychoanalytic theory the prevention of *Id* instincts from reaching conscious recognition and response, because of specific *Ego* controls directed by the *Superego*. 3. In Pavlovian reflexology (a) the submergence of a positive or *excitatory* conditioned reflex by a contrary *inhibitory* one, (b) the supposed occurrence of a radiating inhibitory process over the cerebral cortex controlling the corresponding *neutral reflex arcs*.

INSANITY. A vague *legal* term variously connoting inability "to distinguish right from wrong," or "a mental state in which the patient is unable to care for himself or constitutes a danger to others." To be distinguished from the psychiatric concept of *psychosis* (see p. 212).

INSIGHT. 1. Clinically, the patient's own explanation of his illness, progressively judged "distorted," "incomplete," "good," etc. by the observer in so far as it coincides with his own theoretic formulations. 2. In psychoanalysis, the extent of a patient's true (as opposed to merely "professed" or "verbal") understanding of the origins and unconscious dynamisms of his behavior. 3. In Gestalt psychology, the phenomenon of sudden grasp ("ah-ah!" *erlebnis*) of a perceptual configuration or of the solution to a problem.

INSTINCT. 1. A conative psychologic term with variable meaning, but generally connoting an inborn tendency toward specific patterns of behavior (e.g., the sex instinct, the exploratory instinct, etc.). 2. In older psychoanalytic theory, a primary tendency toward life and reproduction (*Eros*) or toward destruction, dissolution and death (*Thanatos*).

INTELLIGENCE. The sum total and degree of development of the organism's capacities to perceive, differentiate, integrate, and manipulate its environment (Tolman). Spearman contends that there is an overall index (g) of *general* intelligence, plus factors for *perseveration* (p), fluency (f), will (w), and speed (s).

Others divide intelligence into less interdependent capacities: e.g., *abstract i.*, *mechanical i.* and *social i.* (Thorndike), or various special (statistically determined) vectors of intellectual capacity such as *memory* (m), *verbal comprehension* (v), *verbal fluency* (w), *space visualization* (s), *number facility* (n), and, possibly, other factors of *induction*, *deduction*, *speed of reaction*, *perception*, *judgment*, *closure* (including *flexibility*), and *rate of reversal* of ambiguous perceptions (Thurstone). In any case, the ordinary tests of "general intelligence" (e.g., the Stanford-Binet or Kuhlman) indicate only rough averages of these abilities; moreover, they often do not take adequate account of intercurrent conative and affective factors, or of the previous training and experiences of the subject.

INTELLIGENCE QUOTIENT (IQ). A figure indicating the subject's performance on some test of intelligence (see p. 217) in relation to the statistical norm for his age, e.g., a child of 12 (chronological age) whose performance totalled the $8\frac{1}{2}$ year level (mental age) on the Binet–Stanford test would have an IQ of $8\frac{1}{2} \div 12$ or 71. See *intelligence*.

INTUITION. A sudden understanding, or conviction not reached by conscious reasoning; usually an integration of unconscious knowledge that reaches consciousness as an illuminating *insight* or inspiration.

KORSAKOFF PSYCHOSIS. A toxic, organic deterioration (usually alcoholic) characterized by inflammatory or retrogressive changes in peripheral nerves (polyneuritis), disorientation, amnesia with confabulation, and *dementia* (see p. 197).

LIBIDO. 1. In psychoanalytic theory, the energy associated with the instincts of the *Id*. 2. In a more limited (medical and lay) sense the desire for sexual relationships; sex drive.

LOVE. 1. An affect or sentiment evoked by a person, concept, or object that fulfills one's need or expectations. (This definition is not recommended for domestic consumption.) 2. "Love is the effort of two solitudes to protect and touch and greet each other"—Rainer Maria Rilke. Also see *rapport*, *sentiment*, and *infatuation*.

MALINGERING. The deliberate simulation of disease; usually, however, by neurotic individuals.

MANNERISM. A characteristic expression, gesture, or movement. When stereotyped and unconsciously repetitious, but minor, it is termed a tic. Such movements may become symbolically bizarre and persistent in schizophrenia (see p. 215).

MASOCHISM. 1. In sexology, erotic pleasure derived from physical pain. 2. In older psychoanalytic theory, the satisfaction of destructive instincts (*Thanatos*) turned against the self. 3. In biodynamics, the satisfaction of bodily needs through learned adaptive patterns, certain aspects of which may appear unpleasant or painful to an observer.

MECHANISM. 1. In psychoanalytic theory, the mechanics of interaction among psychic "structures": e.g., the *Ego* "defends itself" against the *Id* by the "mechanism" of repression (see pp.33 and 34). 2. In biodynamics, a process of contingent and total organismic *adaptation* devoid of any implication of an isolated pattern.

MELANCHOLIA. A severe depressive psychosis (see p. 212).

MENTAL HYGIENE. A term employed (but not coined) by Meyer to designate the development of optimal modes of personal and social conduct and the prevention of psychiatric disorders.

METAPSYCHOLOGY. A psychological theory that cannot be verified or disproved by observation or reasoning.

MIGRAINE. A disorder characterized by recurrent attacks of severe localized or one-sided (hemicranial) headaches, which are often preceded or accompanied by visual disturbances, gastrointestinal dysfunctions, and physical fatigue or prostration.

MIGRAINE EQUIVALENTS. Various transient paresthesias, motor disturbances, or organic dysfunctions that may replace an attack of *migraine*.

MIND. 1. A generalized abstraction comprising a person's motivations, affects, intelligence, values, beliefs, etc. 2. Operationally, the phenomena of body in internal (including speech) and external action.

MCNAGHTEN RULE. A legal precedent from the murder trial of Daniel McNaghten (England, 1843) to the effect (a) that any act committed by an idiot, imbecile, or lunatic cannot be adjudged a crime; and (b) that such persons cannot be tried and punished by criminal procedure if it can be shown that they were aware neither of the "nature" of their act, nor that it was "wrong." This precedent is still incorporated into the criminal law of twenty-nine of our states.

MORON. 1. A mentally defective person, with average intelligence (IQ) of from 50 (low grade m.) to 79 (high grade m.) as estimated by standard intelligence tests with a "norm" of about a hundred. 2. A lay or journalistic term incorrectly applied to sexual perverts.

MOURNING. A state of grief and sadness over a loss; theoretically distinguished from *depression* or melancholia (see p. 198) by the absence of marked self-recrimination, persistent agitation, a severe depressive syndrome, or suicidal impulses. Compare *psychosis, depressive.*

MULTIPLE (DISSEMINATED) SCLEROSIS. A diffuse, remissive, but generally progressive organic disease of the central nervous system manifested variously by tremor, scanning speech, and *nystagmus* (the Charcot triad), *ataxia*, sensory disturbances and optic atrophy. There may be neurotic or psychotic reactions to these disabilities, or there may be symptoms indicative of organic damage to the brain (see *organic psychoses*).

NARCISSISM. From Narcissus, who, for rejecting the devotion of Echo, was condemned by Nemesis to fall in love with his own reflected image. In psychoanalysis, equivalent to original self-love, or to the reidentification with, or fantasied reincorporation of, objects or persons given a temporary investiture (cathexis) of object-love. The first form is called *primary*, the rederived form *secondary*.

NARCOLEPSY. Recurrent episodes of trance-like or sleep states, occurring with no, or minimal warning, and persisting from a few seconds to several hours. They may be of neurotic etiology; also see epileptic equivalents.

NARCOSYNTHESIS. A therapeutic procedure, particularly applicable to recent combat neuroses, in which the patient is given an hypnotic drug (e.g., Pentothal) to alleviate his acute anxiety, permitted to express his repressed memories, affects, and conflicts (see catharsis) and then guided by the therapist to conative and emotional reintegration, behavioral readjustments, and social rehabilitation. See Sodium Amytal.

NEED. A pyschologic metabolic deficiency or imbalance translated dynamically into behavior (characterized variously as motivated by desires, drives, goals, instincts, wishes, strivings, etc.) directed toward satisfaction of the need.

NERVES, NERVOUS, NERVOUS BREAKDOWN, NERVOUS SPELLS, ETC. Lay euphemisms used vaguely to describe almost any behavior disorder. These terms should not be used, other than in quotes from the patient, in psychiatric description or diagnosis.

NEURASTHENIA. A euphemistic and psychiatrically obsolescent term for a vague group of symptoms consisting of muscular weakness or fatigability, inertia, petulant irritability, aversion to effort, variable aches and pains, and minor organic dysfunctions. At present the term has no connotation of organic disease of the nervous system.

NEUROSES. A group of behavior disorders representing suboptimal adaptations to biodynamic stress and conflict. Neuroses are characterized symptomatically by 1. *anxiety*, with its recurrent physiologic manifestations (see anxiety syndrome), more or less covered 2. by various pervasive *defenses* and *fixations* such as sensorimotor (hysterical) or organ-neurotic (*psychosomatic*) dysfunctions (see p. 102). Generally, the history reveals previous sensitivities and maladaptations to frustration and conflict, exacerbation of neurotic symptomatology under duress, and partial recovery when stress is relieved either spontaneously or under therapy. For theoretic and practical purposes, *neuroses* are distinguished from *psychoses* by the criteria listed under the latter, although all forms of transition occur.

NEUROSIS, CONVERSION. Characterized predominantly by dysfunctions of (a) sensation or motility (*hysteria*), or (b) one or more organ-systems (*organ neurosis*). Frank anxiety or obsessive–compulsive defenses may be minimal, especially when the hysterical symptoms serve as adequate adaptations.

NEUROSIS, OBSESSIVE–COMPULSIVE. Characterized prominently by *obsessions* and *compulsions*, usually combined with *phobias*. When these are transgressed, an acute *anxiety syndrome* occurs (see p. 193).

NIRVANA FANTASY. From the Nirvana of Buddhist theology, a state in which there is no desire, no affect, and no strife—only pervasive peace. Differs from *intrauterine fantasy* in the sense that the latter may connote deeply regressive maternal-cosmic reidentification.

OBSESSION. A persistent, conscious desire or idea, recognized as being more or less irrational by the subject, which usually impels compulsive acts on pain of anxiety if they are not performed. Obsessions can often be analyzed as conscious reflections of unconscious conflictual wishes.

OCCUPATIONAL THERAPY. Treatment by diverting the patient's energies into constructive recreational or manual pursuits satisfactory to him.

ORGASM. The height of erotic pleasure, just preceding detumescence and relaxation. Generally refers to erotic sensations centered in the genitals, but orgastic sensations in the mouth, breast, anus, or even skin (as in masturbatory-equivalent scratching) have been described.

ORIENTATION. Awareness of place, time circumstances, and inter-personal relationships.

ORTHOPSYCHIATRY. The study of the phenomena and dynamisms of the development of "normal" behavior, with emphasis on child psychiatry and "mental hygiene" (see p. 206).

OVERCOMPENSATION. 1. An adaptive process particularly stressed by Alfred Adler, whereby a person overreacts to initial deficiencies, handicaps, or inhibitions in some sphere of activity by becoming exceedingly adept in that field (e.g., Demosthenes, afflicted with an impediment of speech in his youth, strove for, and succeeded in reaching, the pinnacles of oratorical power). 2. In psychoanalytic theory, an excessive overplay of any defense mechanism, e.g., excessive politeness toward a disliked person, or compulsive *satyriasis* (heterosexual extremes) as a defense against unconscious homosexual tendencies.

OVERDETERMINATION. A process whereby a single behavior pattern becomes adaptive to many unconscious needs, thus rendering it particularly fixed and resistant to therapy. For instance, a hysterical paralysis (see p. 105), of an arm may be a combat flier's initial reaction to a crash landing, but later the same symptom may also come to symbolize (a) an unconscious defense against his own mobilized aggressions, (b) a rationalized excuse for not returning to a hated civilian job, (c) expiation for a regressive dependence on a government pension, etc. In this sense, overdetermination parallels the process of *condensation* (see p. 96) in the formation of verbal and dream symbols.

PANIC. Extreme anxiety, with blind flight or marked disorganization of behavior.

PARALYSIS AGITANS (PARKINSON'S DISEASE). An organic disease of the brain, particularly of the basilar nuclei, caused by inflammation (encephalitis), drugs, or senile changes and characterized by progressive muscular dystonia, spasticity and tremor, disturbances in motor control (*festination, retropulsion, dissociation of movement*), and sometimes by outbreaks of irrational rages and excitements.

PARASYMPATHETIC NERVOUS SYSTEM. The cranio–sacral, vagal, cholinergic, and generally anabolic and inhibitory portion of the sympathetic nervous system.

PARESIS (GENERAL PARESIS, GENERAL PARALYSIS OF THE INSANE). An organic psychosis (see p. 213) caused by syphilis of the brain and generally characterized by affective instability with recurrent excitements, muscular tremors, speech disturbances, pathognomic changes in the pupillary reactions and in the spinal fluid, and progressive behavioral deterioration.

PERCEPTION. The integration of sensory stimuli to form an image, the configuration and interpretation of which is influenced by past experiences.

PERSONALITY. Operationally, this term comprises the sum total of the unique behavior patterns of an individual, particularly those concerned in his social relationships.

PERSUASION. In psychiatry, a form of therapeutic influence, usually conceived as verbal, by which the patient's motivations, unconscious as well as conscious, are directed toward goals desired by the therapist.

PHOBIA. A morbid dread of an object, situation, or act, generally derived from its unconsciously symbolic reference to an anxiety-ridden previous experience or series of experiences.

Specific names, derived from Greek roots, for the almost infinite varieties of phobias are rapidly becoming obsolete.

PLEASURE-PRINCIPLE. In psychoanalytic theory, the seeking of release from *libidinal tensions* (giving pleasure) as distinguished from various manifestations of the death-instinct or Thanatos (such as the *repetition-compulsion* and *masochism*).

PREJUDICE. An intellectual set that unconsciously biases or distorts a subject's apperception and evaluation of later experiences according to his predetermined attitudes.

PROJECTION. An unconscious defense process whereby the subject attributes his own motivations, concepts, or acts to others.

PROLONGED SLEEP. Treatment of behavior disorders by continuous sleep (1 to 20 days) induced by drugs such as paraldehyde or Amytal (*Dauerschlaf*).

PSYCHOANALYSIS. A psychologic system of research, theory, and therapy, the broad outlines of which were propounded by Sigmund Freud (1856–1939). (See index for the multiple elaborations and implications of this theory.)

PSYCHOBIOLOGY. An eclectic system of behavior research, theory, and therapy outlined by Adolf Meyer (1866–1944).

PSYCHOLOGY, ANALYTIC. The metapsychology of Carl Jung, distinguished from Freudian psychoanalysis by various quasi-mystic concepts such as those of *anima, persona,* and *racial unconscious* by its rejection of orthodox analytic techniques, and by its emphasis on didactic and inspirational guidance by the analyst.

PSYCHOLOGY, GESTALT. A psychological system (Wertheimer, Koffka, Kohler, *et al.*) that rejects elemental stimulus-response (*reflex*) concepts of behavior, stresses the indivisible wholeness of perceptual configurations (Gestalten), and emphasizes the sudden "insight-ful" nature of learning as opposed to trial-and-error or automatic "association."

PSYCHONEUROSIS. A term now generally used as equivalent to neurosis (see p. 208) or sometimes as implying severe neuroses with larval or minimal psychotic tendencies or admixtures.

PSYCHOSES. A group of grave disorders of behavior, most of which satisfy the legal criteria of insanity in that the patient is unable to care for himself and/or constitutes a danger to others. Psychoses, however, also fulfill one or more of the following psychiatric criteria: (1) loss of contact with, or marked distortion of, socially accepted interpretations of reality (as shown in deviated perceptions, thinking disorders, *hallucinations*, or *delusions*); (2) severe and persistent disorders of affect (e.g., manic *euphoria*, depressive *melancholia*, or schizophrenic emotional blunting and lack of correspondence between *affect* and *idea*); (3) marked regression, with (a) retreat from, or perversion of, social relationships (e.g., perverse passivity, dependency, or aggressivity) or (b) habit reversions (e.g., open masturbation, soiling, etc.); (4) personality disintegration, so that elementary erotic and hostile impulses or automatisms are released from control; and (5) (a) acute derangement of perceptive–interpretative–manipulative ("intellectual") capacities (as in toxic deliria) or (b) the permanent deterioration of such capacities (as in psychoses with organic cerebral disease).

PSYCHOSES, DEPRESSIVE. Psychoses variously characterized by melancholic fixation of mood, retardation of apperception and response, self-depreciatory preoccupations (ideas of inadequacy, of guilt, and of being hated), morbid preoccupations with anticipated punishment, nihilistic fantasies ("all is hopeless," or "lost"), episodes of agitation, petulant demanding helplessness and *regression*, suicidal tendencies, and a marked depressive physiologic *syndrome* comprising insomnia, anorexia, loss of weight, sexual disturbance, and various organic (especially gastrointestinal) dysfunctions.

PSYCHOSES, INVOLUTIONAL. Originally considered to be a definite syndrome characterized mainly by melancholia and agitation, generally progressing to hebetude and intellectual deterioration. Acutally, psychoses occurring in the involutional period vary widely in etiology, clinical expression, and prognosis.

PSYCHOSES, MANIC. A psychosis (see p. 00) characterized by extreme emotional lability (though with superficially euphoric effect), psychomotor hyperactivity (uninhibited flow of free-associative speech and conduct), hypersensitivity to stimuli with marked distractability, and a tendency to unorganized delusions of grandiosity. Manic episodes are generally self-limited in duration; occasionally, they are apt to recur regularly (*cyclic mania*) or, more rarely, in alternation with periods of depression (*manic–depressive psychosis*). Rare cases of *chronic mania* (Schott) have been reported.

PSYCHOSES, ORGANIC. Psychoses (see p. 212) in which pathologic changes in the body, especially in the central nervous system, are etiologically significant contributory factors, e.g., psychoses with pellagra, chronic alcoholism, cerebral tumor, brain syphilis, etc. Organic psychoses are characterized by *dementia* and, generally, by impaired affective control.

PSYCHOSES, PARANOIAC. A relatively rare (about 4 percent incidence) psychosis (see p. 212) characterized by well-systematized, slowly progressive delusions of influence, reference, or persecution, based on false premises and interpretations, but relatively logical and consistent, and accompanied by appropriate affect. Paranoia is distinguished from the affective psychoses and from schizophrenia in that in paranoia there is minimal *affective distortion* or *disintegration*; e.g., the paranoiac system is relatively isolated from the rest of the personality pattern (see schizophrenia, paranoid).

PSYCHOSES, SENILE. Organic psychoses caused by senile degenerative or arteriosclerotic changes in the brain, and generally characterized by progressive dementia (*aphasic* defects, *amnesia* for recent events), habit deteriorations (e.g., loss of cultural interests, garrulity, hoarding, personal uncleanliness), and regressions to puerile affectivity (e.g., the petulant dependence and selfishness of "second childhood"). See Alzheimer's disease.

PSYCHOSOMATIC MEDICINE. The study, theory, and application of the dynamics of total behavior (biodynamics) in relation to the practice of medicine and its several specialities.

PSYCHOTHERAPY. The science and art of influencing behavior so as to make it (a) more compatible with social norms, (b) more efficient and satisfactory to the individual.

RATIONALIZATION. The conscious justification (usually on grounds of "reason," "logic," or social expediency) of attitudes, concepts, and acts after these have already been determined by unconscious motivations.

REACTION, FORMATION. In psychoanalytic theory, the process whereby conscious wishes, affects, ideation, or behavior are made defensively contrary to rejected unconscious impulses, e.g., a father's overt cruelty to a daughter to whom, unconsciously, he is incestuously attracted.

REACTION-TYPE. In psychobiology (A. Meyer), designates the predominant behavior pattern or ergasia of a psychiatric patient: i.e., *anergasia* (intellectually defective), *dysergasia* (toxic), *pathergasia* (organic), *holergasia* (psychotic), *meregasia* (neurotic part-reaction), *oligergasia* (feeble-minded), *parergasia* (schizophrenic), and *thymergasia* (affective psychoses).

REALITY-PRINCIPLE. In psychoanalytic theory, the modification of the expression of unconscious libidinal drives (*Eros* or *pleasure-principle*) or of the death-instincts (*Thanatos* or the *Nirvana-principle*) by rational consideration of the requirements of "reality."

REFERENCE, DELUSION OF. A fixed, irrational belief that one is the object of the thoughts and actions of others.

REFLEX. In neurophysiology, a sensorimotor neural pathway. See *conditioning* and Index for other connotations of the term.

REGRESSION. 1. The resumption, under stress, of earlier and experientially more satisfactory modes of behavior. 2. In psychoanalytic theory, the return to infantile phases of *libidinal organization*, i.e., *narcissistic, oral,* or *anal*.

REPRESSION. The automatic and unconsciously defensive process of banishing dangerous desires, affects, or ideas, singly or together, from awareness to the unconscious, distinguished from suppression in which the control exercised is seemingly deliberate and conscious.

RESISTANCE. In psychiatric, and especially psychoanalytic, therapy the reluctance (mainly unconscious) of the patient to relinquish accustomed patterns of thinking, feeling, and acting, however neurotic, in favor of new and untried modes of adaptation. In psychoanalytic theory resistance often has the more limited meaning of the *Ego's* refusal to accept insight into the *Unconscious*, as shown by the patient's covert rejection of interpretation or the development of a *negative transference* (see p. 219).

SCHIZOPHRENIA. A group of variable psychotic syndromes characterized predominantly by (a) general blunting and distortion of affect, especially in relation to professed ideational content and interpersonal relationships; (b) bizarre perceptual and category formations and thinking disturbances, loosely organized into fantastic delusional systems, and sometimes projected as hallucinatory experiences; (c) regression to primitive forms of narcissistic, erotic or aggressive expression; and (d) disintegration of behavior with the appearance of stereotypes and motor automatisms (see p. 81 and p. 194). For the various clinical forms of schizophrenia, see below.

SCHIZOPHRENIA, CATATONIC. Characterized by motor disturbances (catalepsy, *flexibilitas cerea, negativism, mannerisms*), stupors or acute outbreaks of hallucinatory excitement, and occasional periods of remission.

SCHIZOPHRENIA, HEBEPHRENIC. A highly variable form, particularly characterized by early onset, insidious distortion and blunting of affect, inconstant hallucinosis and fragmentary delusional formations, the development of symbolic mannerisms and *stereotypes*, and progressive deterioration of personal and social habits (Kahlbaum, Kraepelin).

SCHIZOPHRENIA, LATENT. Schizoid or schizophrenic tendencies likely to find overt expression under unfavorable stress.

SCHIZOPHRENIA, PARANOID. A form in which delusions of reference and influence are prominent, distinguished from paranoia in that (a) the delusions are highly fantastic, logically bizarre, and poorly systematized, and (b) other schizophrenic criteria (affect distortion, pervasive behavioral disintegration, etc.) are also present. See paranoia.

SCHIZOPHRENIA, PROCESS. A term sometimes used to designate schizophrenic "dementia" in which organic changes in the brain are found or are postulated to be important etiologic factors.

SCHIZOPHRENIA, PSEUDONEUROTIC. Ambulatory schizophrenia underlying severe hysterical, somatic, obsessive–compulsive–phobic, or character neuroses ( Hoch, Rado).

SCHIZOPHRENIC DETERIORATION. Disintegration of habit patterns and disuse of intellectual capacities consequent on schizophrenic contraction of interests and deviations or perversions of behavior; however, except in so-called *process* (organic) schizophrenia, there is no demonstrable loss of basic abilities.

SCREEN-MEMORY. 1. A relatively acceptable memory recalled in place of one charged (cathected) with greater anxiety. 2. A retrospective illusion.

SHOCK-TREATMENT. The subjection of psychiatric patients to convulsive doses of Metrazol, carbon dioxide, or insulin, or to electric current passed through the brain.

SOCIOPATH, SOCIOPATHIC PERSONALITY. Generally refers to an individual who is not readily classifiable as predominantly intellectually defective, *autoplastically* neurotic, or definitely *psychotic* but whose behavior is characterized by recurrently episodic impulsivity, irresponsibility, lack of emotional control, and inadequate or unstable educational, marital, occupational, and other social adaptations. Sociopaths are prone to come into conflict with police or other authorities—a tendency used by some to distinguish them from a group of "neurotic characters" who keep their eccentricities and aberrations (e.g., prejudices, excessive religiosity, obsessive–compulsive–phobic behavior, etc.) within the bounds of law and custom. Formerly psychopathic personality.

SUBLIMATION. A "normal" process of deviating unconscious and essentially selfish motivations into socially acceptable services or creative activities.

SUBSTITUTION. The replacement of conations, affects, concepts, or acts by others with a lesser charge of anxiety.

SUGGESTION. A process of gestural or verbal communication by which one person may use another's evaluations of him (see *transference* relations) to channelize the other's behavior into desired patterns.

SUPEREGO. In psychoanalytic theory, that portion or function of the personality that (a) as *conscience*, prohibits the *Ego* from direct forms of instinct-expression and thereby prompts various defense mechanisms against unconscious *Id* impulses, and (b) as *Ego-ideal*, channelizes behavior along patterns similar to those of individuals with whom the subject wished to identify (i.e., whose advantages he unconsciously desires).

SUPPRESSION. The conscious subjugation and control of impulses, ideas, affects, and acts felt to be dangerous.

SYMBOL. The more or less remotely displaced representation of an experience in imagery.

SYMPATHETIC NERVOUS SYSTEM. That portion of the nervous system that innervates the organs and glands of the body, as dis-distinguished from the peripheral nerves that innervate the muscles and sense organs. Usually divided functionally into the *orthosympathetic* n.s. (generally catabolic) and the *parasympathetic* n.s. (generally anabolic).

TEST. Any controlled or standardized situation for investigating the behavior patterns of a subject. Tests frequently referred to in the literature are here grouped as to the field of behavior tested:

INTELLIGENCE TESTS—

*Cattell Infant Intelligence Scale.* Performance levels for infants from 2 to 30 months of age. Scored like the Stanford–Binet (see below).

*Kuhlman Intelligence Test.* Stresses performance over verbal facility and is therefore more accurate in the presence of language difficulties than is the Stanford–Binet. Measures also rate of development, speed, and accuracy.

*Otis Self-Administering.* Four alternate forms for rough estimate of average perceptive-integrative capacity, especially as to speed and alertness.

*Stanford–Binet* (revised). Test items are arranged in year levels from 2 to superior adult. The level at which the subject passes all items is the basal year; his total score is his mental age; this divided by his chronological age (up to 16) is his intelligence quotient. Tests results are most accurate for privileged children, but not reliable for adults unless contingently interpreted. The "normal" range is from 90 to 109; other ranges are: 0–24, idiot; 25–49, imbecile (both requiring custodial care); 50–69, moron, requiring special extramural supervision; 70–79, borderline; 80–89, dull normal; 110–124, superior; 125–139, very superior; 140, maximal. Wide ranges of performance and failures in abstract items may indicate organic deterioration.

*Wechsler–Bellevue Intelligence Scale.* A verbal and performance test, standardized on adults, that investigates information, comprehension, arithmetical reasoning, digit memory, similarities, configurational grasp, visual completion, and object assembly; or, as an alternate test, the subject's vocabulary, Subtests are weighted for speed and accuracy, and differentially graded. IQ as in estimating average intelligence in adults.

PROJECTIVE TESTS—

These study the subject's "projected" imagery, static or kinetic, in response to standard stimuli (see projection). The most frequently used are these:

*Rorschach Psychodiagnostic Experiment.* The subject describes what he sees on a series of ten standard cards showing large, almost symmetrical inkblots, five black and white and five colored. His answers are graded as to *form* (F), *movement* (M), *color* (C), and other criteria as to *whole fieldperception* (W), *detail organization* (D or d), *"color shock,"* *chiaroscuro effects* (K), *banal* (P) or *original* (O) content, etc. Scoring indicates personality patterns (e.g., *"pedantry"*), special interests, and (less reliably) general intelligence; in addition the patient's performance may reveal deviations of affect, and neurotic or psychotic tendencies. The administration and evaluation of the Rorschach test requires special training and skill, else its reported results may be seriously misleading.

*Szondi Test.* The subject's expressed preferences among a series of photographs is held to be psychiatrically diagnostic; highly dubious rationale and reliability.

*Thematic Apperception Test.* The subject is shown twenty photographs of various dramatic scenes and is asked to tell a story about each. These stories may then be analyzed (1) as to their themes of opposed motivations and frustrations (Morgan and Murray), or (2) their symbolic significance as to the subject's unconscious conflicts and their verbal content of various expressions, words, or phrases indicating underlying anxiety, doubt, or depression as opposed to wishfully defensive fantasy patterns (Masserman and Balken). The evaluation of this test, too, requires extensive psychiatric training and special experience on the part of the examiner.

THERAPY. In psychiatry, the science, techniques and art of exerting a favorable influence on behavior disorders by every ethical means available. (See index.)

TRANSFERENCE. 1. In general, the attribution (transfer) of desires, feelings, and relationships, originally experienced by the subject with regard to his parents and siblings, onto other persons who, in the subject's residual unconscious attitudes, take on reassigned parental or other familial roles in his later life. 2. More specifically in psychoanalytic therapy, the unconscious attitude of the patient toward the analyst and the role in which the latter is fantasied, e.g., maternal, rivalrous, erotic, etc.

TYPES OF CHARACTER, PERSONALITY OR PHYSIQUE. The various classifications are legion, but the following are most often referred to in the literature:

Draper, G.—

The hereditary characteristics of an individual (biotype as derived from genotype), further modified by environment (phenotype).

Galenic–Hippocratic (humoral)—

1. *Choleric* (dominated by "yellow bile"): mercurial, irritable, impulsive.
2. *Melancholic* (dominated by "black bile"): brooding, emotional depressive.
3. *Phlegmatic* (dominated by "phlegm"): slow, apathetic, stolid.
4. *Sanguine* (dominated by "strong blood"): impulsive, active, optimistic.

Hippocratic—

1. *Habitus Apoplecticus:* Thick-set, heavy body-build, susceptible to apoplexy.
2. *Habitus phthisicus:* Tall, slender, angular body-build, susceptible to pulmonary disease.

Jaensch, E. R.—

1. *B:* Basedow, or integrated constitution, characterized by a capacity for voluntary control of vivid *eidetic imagery*, a tendency to hyperthyroidism, relatively stable emotional organization and a typical end-capillary structure.

2. *T:* tetanic or unintegrated constitution, distinguished by lesser control of imagery, low blood calcium, hypersensitivity to stimuli and dissociated personality reactions. Recent work indicates that the Jaensch typology, especially that concerned with its racial implications, has very little scientific validity.

Jung, C.—

1. *Introverted:* self-concerned, ruminative, remote, imaginative, inclined to schizoid behavior (Kretschmer).

2. *Extroverted:* objective, sensitive to external affairs, emotionally labile, active, energetic; inclined to manic-depressive disorders.

3. *Feeling types:* labile and sensitive affect.

4. *Intuitive types:* markedly influenced by their unconscious racial and personal heritage.

Kretschmer, E.—

1. *Asthenic or leptosomic:* a body type characterized by leanness, underweight, flat chest, and underdeveloped muscular system, especially marked in the phthisoid subgroup.

2. *Athletic:* characterized by robust skeletal and muscular development; generally schizothymic.

3. *Dysplastic:* a group of "body-types" that show wide anthropometric deviations from the other three types and that also tend to schizothymia.

4. *Pyknic:* short, stocky, large body cavities, bradycephalic; inclined to cyclothymia.

Sheldon, W.—

1. *Ectomorphic:* a "body-type" characterized by predominant development of the ectoderm (epidermis, sense organs, and central nervous system), hence sensitive and hyperreactive.

2. *Endomorphic:* predominant endoderm derivatives (mainly gastrointestinal and organic), hence interest in nutritive living.

3. *Mesomorphic:* predominantly skeletal and muscular, hence active and energetic. All persons are classified as a mixture of these fundamental "types," graded as to predominance on a scale of 1 to 7.

Stockard, C. R.—

1. "Lateral" as distinguished from
2. "Linear" body-types.

Viola, G.—

1. *Microsplanchnic:* a "body-type" with small viscera and well-developed soma, as distinguished from

2. *Macrosplanchnic:* corresponding to the pyknic. (See Kretschmer.)

3. *Normosplanchnic or Eumorphic* designates a normal intermediate or optimal "body-type."

UNCONSCIOUS. 1. In general, any behavioral process of which the subject is not directly aware. 2. In psychoanalytic topography, that portion of the psyche that comprises the *Id* instincts, plus those large parts of the *Ego* (adaptive) and *Superego* (self-directive) portions of the personality that are in contact with the *Id*, and the functions of which are not available to direct awareness (*consciousness*) or immediate recall and introspection (*preconscious*). 3. In addition, unconscious has many meanings as variously used in the literature, ranging from stuporous to vaguely mystic connotations of atavistic communality (Jung, Miller).

UNDOING. A defensive reversal of an anxiety-ridden act.

UR-DEFENSES (-DELUSIONS, -ILLUSIONS). Irrational but indestructible faiths in one's own (1) physical powers, (2) supposed friends, and (3) magic concepts and practices.

WORKING-THROUGH. 1. In general, an active reexploration of a problem situation until satisfactory solutions or adaptations are found and firmly established. (2) In psychoanalysis, the tracing of a *symbolism* to its "deepest" unconscious sources.

# References

For more detailed and technical discussions of the topics surveyed in this book, and for over two thousand references to relevant publications, consult the following texts by the author of this treatise:

*Practice of Dynamic Psychiatry*, Philadelphia, W. B. Saunders, 1955.

*Principles of Dynamic Psychiatry*, Philadelphia, W.B. Saunders, Ed. 2, 1961.

*Modern Concepts of Psychoanalysis* (with L. Salzman). New York, Philosophical Library, 1962.

*Behavior and Neurosis*. New York, Hafner & Co., 1963.

*Biodynamic Roots of Human Behavior*. Springfield, Illinois, Charles C Thomas, 1968.

*A Psychiatric Odyssey*. New York, Science House, 1970.

*Man for Humanity* (with J. Schwab). Springfield, Illinois, Charles C Thomas, 1972.

*Handbook of Psychiatric Therapies*. New York, Science House, 1973.

# Bibliography

## Adolescence

ERIKSON, E. H. *Childhood and Society.* New York: W. W. Norton & Co., 1950.

TSUNG-YI, L. "Social Change and Mental Health." *World Mental Health* 12 (1960): 65.


## Aging

ANDERSON, J. E., ed. *Pschological Aspects of Aging.* Washington, D.C.: American Psychological Assn. 1956.

FROMM-REICHMANN, Frieda. "Loneliness." *Psychiatry* 22 (1959): 1-15.


## Anxiety

BASOWITZ, L., *et al. Anxiety and Stress.* New York: McGraw-Hill and Co., 1955.

FREUD, S. *The Problem of Anxiety.* New York: W. W. Norton & Co., 1936.

KIERKEGAARD, S. *The Concept of Dread.* Princeton, New Jersey: Princeton University Press, 1944.

SARBIN, T. R. "Anxiety: Reification of a Metaphor." *Arch. Gen. Psychiat.* 10 (1964): 630.


## Childhood

BOWLBY, J. *Maternal Care and Mental Health.* Geneva: WHO. Mono. Series, 1952.

CHESS, STELLA, *et al.* "Implications of Longitudinal Study of Child Development." *Am. J. Psychiat.* 117 (1960): 439.

KLEIN, MELANIE. *The Psychoanalysis of Children.* London: Hogarth Press, 1937.

LIPPMAN, H. S. *Treatment of the Child in Emotional Conflict.* New York: McGraw-Hill and Co., 1956.

MASLAND, R. L.; SARASON, S. B.; and GLADIVIN, T. *Mental Subnormality.* New York: Basic Books, 1958.

NORRIS, A. S. "Prenatal Factors in Intellectual and Emotional Development." *J. A. M. A.* 172 (1960): 413.


## Community

BELLAK, L., ed. *Handbook of Community Psychiatry.* New York: Grune & Stratton, 1964.

## Existentialism

JASPERS, K. *Reason and Existence*. New York: Noonday Publ. Co., 1955.

KIERKEGAARD, S. *The Concept of God*. Princeton: Princeton University Press, 1944.

SONNEMAN, U. *Existence and Therapy*. New York: Grune & Stratton, 1954.

## General and Philosophic

DEUTSCH, A. and FISHMAN, H., eds. *Encyclopedia of Mental Health*. New York: Franklin Watts, Inc., 1963.

MONTAGU, M. F. ASHLEY. *Man and Aggression*. New York: Oxford University Press, 1968.

NIEBUHR, R. *The Self and the Dramas of History*. New York: Scribner and Co., 1955.

PASCAL, B. *Thoughts*. New York: Peter Pauper Press, 1946.

POPPER, K. *The Logic of Scientific Discovery*. New York: Philosophical Library, 1958.

ROE, ANN, and SIMPSON, G.G. *Behavior and Evolution*. New Haven: Yale University Press, 1958.

RUESCH, J. *Disturbed Communication*. New York: W. W. Norton & Co., 1957.

SMITH, H. *Man and His Gods*. Boston: Little, Brown and Co., 1957.

SPINOZA, B. *Ethics*. London: Everyman, 1910.

## History

ALEXANDER, F., and SELESNIK, S. *History of Psychiatry*. New York: Harper & Row, 1966.

MASSERMAN, J. H. *A Psychiatric Odyssey*. New York: Science House 1970.

## Methods of Therapy

BERNE, E. *Transactional Analysis in Psychotherapy*. New York: Grove Press, 1961.

EHRENWALD, J. *Psychotherapy: Myth and Method*. New York: Grune & Stratton, 1966.

FRANK, J. D. *Persuasion and Healing*. Baltimore: Johns Hopkins Press, 1961.

GLASS, A. J. "Psychotherapy in the Combat Zone." *Am. J. Psychiat.* 110 (1959): 725.

HALEY, J. *Strategies of Psychotherapy*. New York and London: Grune & Stratton, 1963.

HORNEY, KAREN. *The Neurotic Personality of Our Time*. New York: W. W. Norton & Co., 1937.

KIEV, A. *Magic, Faith and Healing*. New York: Free Press of Glencoe, 1964.

LEIGHTON, A.; CLAUSEN, J.; and WILSON, R. *Explorations in Social Psychiatry*. New York: Basic Books, 1957.

MONROE, R. L. *Schools of Psychoanalytic Thought*. New York: Dryden Press, 1955.

PHILLIPS, E. L. *Psychotherapy: A Modern Theory and Practice*. London: Staples, 1957.

RINKEL, M. *Biological Treatment of Mental Illness*. New York: L. C. Page & Co., 1966.

STEIN, M. I., ed. *Contemporary Psychotherapies*. New York: Free Press of Glencoe, 1961.

WOLBERG, L. *Hypnotherapy*. New York: Grune & Stratton, 1964.

——. *Short-term Psychotherapy*. New York: Grune & Stratton, 1965.

WOLPE, J. *The Practice of Behavior Therapy*. New York: Pergamon Press, 1969.

## Psychiatry

FREEDMAN, A. M., and KAPLAN, H. I. *Comprehensive Textbook of Psychiatry*. Baltimore: Williams and Wilkins, 1967.

## Psychoanalysis

BAKAN, D. *Freud and the Hassidic Tradition*. Chicago: U. of Chicago Press, 1962.

BIEBER, I. "A Critique of Libido Theory." *Am. J. Psychoanal.* 18 (1958): 52.

FREUD, ANNA. *The Ego and the Mechanisms of Defense*. New York: International Universities Press, 1946.

FREUD, S. *Basic Writings*. New York: Modern Library, 1938.

——. *New Introductory Lectures*. New York: W. W. Norton & Co., 1963.

MARMOR, J., ed. *Modern Psychoanalysis*. New York: Basic Books, 1967.

SALZMAN, L., and MASSERMAN, J. H., eds. *Modern Concepts of Psychoanalysis*. New York: Philosophical Library, 1962.

## Sexuality

BARD, L., "Neural Mechanisms in Emotional and Sexual Behavior." *Psychosom. Med.* 4 (1942): 171.

MARMOR, J., ed. *Sexual Inversion*. New York: Basic Books, 1965.

## Systems Theory

GRAY, W.; DEIHL, F. J.; and RIZZO, N. D. *General Systems Theory and Psychiatry*. Boston: Little, Brown & Co., 1969.

## Annual Reviews

MASSERMAN, J. H., ed. *Current Psychiatric Therapies*. Annual Volumes. New York: Grune & Stratton, 1960-.

——. *Science and Psychoanalysis*. Annual Volumes. New York: Grune & Stratton, 1957.

——. and SCHWAB, J. *Social Psychiatry*. Annual Volumes. New York: Grune & Stratton, 1972-.

# Index of Authors

# Index of Subjects

233